DEEPER CONVERSION

God bless you!
Sr. Ann

DEEPER CONVERSION

Extraordinary Grace
for Ordinary Times

SISTER ANN SHIELDS, S.G.L

SERVANT
BOOKS

PUBLISHED BY ST. ANTHONY MESSENGER PRESS
CINCINNATI, OHIO

Cover design by Candle Light Studios
Cover image ©Photodisc
Book design by Mark Sullivan

LIBRARY OF CONGRESS CATALOGING-IN-PUBLICATION DATA
Shields, Ann.
Deeper conversion : extraordinary grace for ordinary times / Ann Shields.
p. cm.
Includes bibliographical references.
ISBN 978-0-86716-811-2 (pbk. : alk. paper) 1. Bible. N.T. Matthew—
Meditations. 2. Spirituality—Catholic Church. 3. Christian life—Catholic
authors. I. Title.

BS2575.54.S55 2008
242'.5—dc22

2007047975

ISBN 978-0-86716-811-2

Published by Servant Books, an imprint of St. Anthony Messenger Press.
28 W. Liberty St.
Cincinnati, OH 45202
www.ServantBooks.org

Printed in the United States of America
Printed on acid-free paper

08 09 10 11 12 5 4 3 2

On life's journey, which is neither easy nor free of deceptions, you will meet difficulties and suffering and at times you will be tempted to exclaim with the psalmist: "I am severely afflicted" (Psalm 119:107). Do not forget to add as the psalmist did: "give me life, O Lord, according to your word...." The loving presence of God, through his word, is the lamp that dispels the darkness of fear and lights up the path even when times are most difficult.

—Pope Benedict XVI
Message to Youth
World Youth Day 2006

. . .

Contents

Introduction

. . .

GOD'S HOLY WORD

AS I PREPARED TO WRITE THIS BOOK, I THOUGHT OF ALL OF YOU to whom I have ministered through conferences, retreats and parish missions; through TV, radio and the Internet. Over the last thirty-five years, in thirty-seven different countries, I have tried to help people know the love of Jesus Christ and follow his Word. I wanted to write this book for you, because my sense is that a very difficult time lies ahead for us, in society and in the Church, signs of which we already see.

I've been praying for myself, that my faith may not fail me, but I have also prayed for all of you to whom I have ministered. I've asked myself, what responsibility do I have to prepare you for what lies ahead? What is it that is most important?

A recent editorial in *The Catholic World Report* points to some of the challenges facing Christians today:

> Western history is moving out along the lines Pope Benedict XVI suggested in his pre-conclave sermon, revolving around the struggle between an increasingly despotic man-centered culture and the God-centered one from which the West came. As the secular West girds itself against an encroaching dictatorship from the Muslim world, it blindly sustains a dictatorship of its own; it worries about losing freedom to the terrorists, then robs God-given liberty from Westerners in the name of its own skewed ideology.

If the dictatorship of relativism succeeds—if all who enter the public square are eventually forced to submit to secularism's inversion of morality—Western culture will have vanished long before the arrival of Islamic terrorists. The Church is nothing less than the West's last hope.[1]

The last sentence here is particularly telling: "The Church is...the West's last hope." And what has the Church taught us? What has the Church upheld through very, very difficult times, over thousands of years?

That teaching is very effectively summarized in the *Catechism of the Catholic Church,* a book I encourage you to keep by your side. My contribution is not to add to that teaching but to spotlight, through Scripture, certain things that Christians need to hold on to in this modern day.

Truths to Hold Firm

The first thing we need to hold on to is our dignity as sons and daughters of God. When we were baptized, we were washed clean in the waters of the font and made children of God. That relationship with God is more real than the earthly families from which we came. We have a dignity that is unparalleled, a dignity for which God himself came to earth, taught, lived, suffered and died.

Saint Paul tells us, "All who are led by the Spirit of God are sons of God. For you did not receive the spirit of slavery to fall back into fear, but you have received the spirit of sonship. When we cry, 'Abba! Father!' it is the Spirit himself bearing witness with our spirit that we are children of God, and if children, then heirs, heirs of God and fellow heirs with Christ, provided we suffer with him in order that we may also be glorified with him" (Romans 8:14–17).

You are of the royal family of the Messiah. That is the truth about who you are and why God, at every moment of every hour of every day and every night, works for your salvation, works that you might inherit the kingdom forever. Don't lose sight of your dignity. Don't let the world nibble away at it or skew it or dilute it. Take hold of your dignity as a son or daughter of God, with both hands!

The next thing to hold on to is the fact that God has destined us to live forever. Saint Paul tells us, "If the Spirit of him who raised Jesus from the dead dwells in you, he who raised Christ Jesus from the dead will give life to your mortal bodies also through his Spirit who dwells in you" (Romans 8:11).

We cannot imagine what that moment was like when Christ broke from the tomb, glorious, never to die again. And that's going to happen to us! By the same Holy Spirit we are destined to live forever. That's fantastic!

Don't let anyone rob you of this truth by pointing out your sin, your weakness, your failure. For another gift God gives us is the forgiveness of our sin. In the midst of our mistakes, our treacheries, our immorality, God gives us a way back. He promises to forgive us; he tells us so clearly in Psalm 103:

[He] forgives *all* your iniquity,
   …heals *all* your diseases,
…redeems your life from the Pit,
   …crowns you with mercy and compassion,
…satisfies you with good as long as you live
   …so that your youth is renewed like the eagle's.…
The LORD is merciful and gracious,
   …slow to anger, and *abounding* in mercy.
He will not always chide,
   …nor will he keep his anger for ever.

He does not deal with us according to our sins,
   nor repay us according to our iniquities.
For as the heavens are high above the earth,
   so great is his mercy toward those who fear him;
as far as the east is from the west,
   so far does he remove our transgressions from us.
As a father pities his children,
   so the LORD pities those who fear him.
For he knows our frame;
   he remembers that we are dust.

(Psalm 103:3–5, 8–14, emphasis mine)

God has done for us what we cannot do for ourselves. Note that the psalm does not say that he forgives *some* of our iniquity, that he heals *some* of our disease. He forgives *all*, and he heals *all*. He redeems and restores *all* those who turn to him and repent of their wrongdoing with their whole heart. Hang on to this truth. Place your hope in God, not in your own righteousness.

OUR PART: OBEDIENCE

God is calling us to express thanksgiving for all that we have been given: our dignity as sons and daughters of God, eternal life and forgiveness of our sins. We express this thanksgiving by living according to his purpose, *by obeying his will.* Psalm 103 also says:

The mercy of the LORD is from everlasting to everlasting
   upon those who fear him,
   and his righteousness to children's children,
to *those who keep his covenant,*
   and remember to *do his commandments.*

(Psalm 103:17–18, emphasis mine)

One of the false notions that plagues our society today is that if obedience is valid at all, it is only for small children who have yet to learn enough about life to be on their own. The common thought among adults is "I can do what I want, how I want, when I want. I've studied; I've graduated; nobody is going to tell me how to run my life." Sound familiar?

This arrogance and pride militate against who we really are and how we were created to live. Now, sometimes we get stuck in such attitudes because of people who have hurt us. But we have to decide to embrace God's purpose in creating us rather than allowing our lives to be controlled by the sins of others.

Sometimes it is not rebellion and arrogance but our good works that build a barrier to a deeper relationship with the Lord. "I teach catechism classes," or "I serve in the prison," or "I am a priest, a religious," and so on. We think our good works and titles will gain God's approval. But God says, "This is the man to whom I will look, he that is humble and contrite in spirit, and trembles at my word" (Isaiah 66:2).

A passage in the First Book of Samuel (see 1 Samuel 15) had a profound effect on my life. In this passage the prophet Samuel severely reprimands Saul for not obeying God's direction. God had told Saul to destroy the Amalekites and all that they had. But Saul took their king alive and then allowed his soldiers to bring back the best of the spoil, ostensibly to use as sacrifice to God in thanksgiving for the victory.

On the face of it, you could say that Saul was kind in sparing the defeated king and that he used the spoil of battle to do good. Yes, but he was not obedient. Samuel tells Saul how God sees his actions:

> Has the LORD as great delight in burnt offerings and
>   sacrifices,
>   as in obeying the voice of the LORD?
> Behold, to obey is better than sacrifice,
>   and to listen than the fat of rams.
> For rebellion is as the sin of divination [witchcraft],
>   and stubbornness is as iniquity and idolatry.
>
> *(1 Samuel 15:22–23)*

That word was like a sword going through my heart, challenging my pride and arrogance. How many times have I chosen my will over God's will?

God is asking us to lay down whatever keeps us from a closer relationship with him—whether it be our rebellion *or* our works. One of the greatest helps he has given us to do precisely that is his Word. We need to study God's Word, not just with our heads but with our hearts. We need to open our spirits to desire to be conformed to God's will. Pope John Paul II said, "Above all, we can pray and be docile to the Holy Spirit and his inspirations."[2] Then we can live in the power of the Holy Spirit, as genuine sons and daughters of God. This is what I call extraordinary grace in ordinary time.

PONDER THE WORD OF GOD

We have a lot of reading material available to us today: fiction and nonfiction books, magazines and newspapers. Then we have input from TV and radio and the Internet. All of this is material with which we can agree or disagree, which we can accept or reject. But we should approach the Bible in a totally different way, for the Bible is the Word of God!

The Bible has power to separate joints and marrow (see

Hebrews 4:12). In other words, the Bible has the power to convict us and to challenge us to the depths of our souls—to bring us to deeper conversion. It can comfort and console and strengthen. All of this comes from the living Holy Spirit, who enlivens the Word with power to direct our lives. No other reading material can give a tenth of that return.

When we open our hearts to the living Word, we open our lives to the living Christ. He will teach and admonish us, challenge and convict us, and he will raise us up and bring us to the fullness of life! One who regularly "feeds" on the Eucharist and on the Word is equipped to live according to God's mind and his Spirit. Our ears become sharper, our hearts softer, our vision clearer.

But many Catholics are on a starvation diet when it comes to the Word of God. They barely hear the Word at Sunday Mass because of internal and external distractions. They rarely ponder the Word or even read it during the week. When some difficulty comes into their lives, they have nothing to cling to and no strength within.

So how do we make the Word of God part of our daily lives?

Pope Benedict XVI stated: "'Spiritual reading' of Sacred Scripture…consists in [poring] over a biblical text for some time, reading and rereading it, 'ruminating' on it as the Fathers say and squeezing from it…all its 'juice,' so that it may nourish meditation and contemplation and, like water, succeed in irrigating life itself."[3]

When I pick up the Bible, it is as though I am holding a beating heart in my hands. I kiss it because, in a certain sense, it is the Word made flesh, the Word spoken from his Spirit to mine. I can count on the Holy Spirit to teach me the deeper meaning of the passage I read, be it a challenge or a conviction or a word of comfort. My meditative reading and study of the Word of God do not just give me information or feed my intellect; the goal is to change my life, to challenge my heart, my spirit and my emotions. God gives me the Bible to feed and strengthen me on the path of truth, on the way that leads to life.

You too can read the Bible with this mind-set. The important thing to remember is to *take your time.* Ponder the Word, as Mary did (see Luke 1:29; 2:19, 51).

In this book I offer meditations on the Gospel readings for the Sundays of Ordinary Time in Year A. Now, the Church uses the term "Ordinary Time" to distinguish the majority of the year from the special seasons of Advent, Christmas, Lent and Easter. But in the power of God's Word, no time is really ordinary. The gift of God's Word is always extraordinary, because it has the power to change our lives. It helps us pursue holiness. If we yield to that power, we can become saints: We can consistently come into deeper and deeper union with Christ Jesus as sons and daughters of God.

I urge you to ponder the meditations in this book carefully; I suggest that you take a week for each one. "Ruminate" on the Word, as Pope Benedict urges, squeezing the "juice" from it. Take a verse or two daily, and see what God is saying to you, what direction he is giving for your life. I pray that as you do, you will find God's extraordinary grace to live a truly holy life, even in the midst of the most ordinary circumstances.

GOSPEL MEDITATIONS

1

. . .

One Like Us

Then Jesus came from Galilee to the Jordan to John, to be baptized by him. John would have prevented him, saying, "I need to be baptized by you, and do you come to me?" But Jesus answered him, "Let it be so now; for thus it is fitting for us to fulfil all righteousness." Then he consented. And when Jesus was baptized, he went up immediately from the water, and behold, the heavens were opened and he saw the Spirit of God descending like a dove, and alighting on him; and behold, a voice from heaven, saying, "This is my beloved Son, with whom I am well pleased."

(Matthew 3:13–17)

In this scene God tells us a lot about his Son *and* about us. Notice that the passage begins with the word *then.* So what we read here comes after something that is connected. Take your Bible and look at the earlier verses.

John has been preaching a call to repentance, and many have been listening. He has declared the coming of the Messiah. This Messiah is so great that John is not even worthy to unfasten his sandals. John preaches the need for people to repent of their sin, so that with the blocks out of the way, they will be able to recognize the Messiah.

John's message is causing quite a stir. People from all walks of life and occupations are following him. Many public sinners are among them, as well as the poor, the sick, the weak, the blind and the lame. Others who hear him probably are turned off by the noise, the dirt, the stench of unwashed bodies. They do not want to be contaminated by sin and human suffering. Yet the crowds around John increase.

Now, John doesn't get bowled over by his popularity. He knows his mission: He was created to be a signpost, to point out the Messiah. On this particular day that the Gospel records, he fearlessly attacks the scribes and the Pharisees, condemning them for their hypocrisy. He calls them, too, to repent.

Suddenly Jesus shows up in their midst, seemingly one more human being in this vast crowd. And he asks to be baptized. We see Jesus, right in the midst of sinful humanity, participating fully in our human life. This is a powerful image to ponder. Our Savior became like us in all things but sin (see Hebrews 4:15). He took on our humanity and walked with us. Now he stands as one of us, asking to be baptized. He is taking on the whole weight of our humanity—all our sin, weakness and stubbornness—that we might have the power to see our sin and repent!

John knows that his cousin is holy, and he is dumbfounded. He says in effect, "What are you doing? I should be baptized by you." And Jesus' reply seems to be, "Let it be. We need to do the Father's will."

John, without fully understanding, submits. He baptizes the pure, all-holy One in obedience to the Father. When Jesus rises from the water, the heavens part. The Spirit of God, in the form of a dove, comes down and alights on Jesus, and we hear the words, "This is my beloved Son, with whom I am well

4

pleased." At this moment a way is made for you and me to have full access to the Father through Jesus by the power of his Spirit.

But often we walk around like orphans. We fail to acknowledge our Father; we fail to take the path he gives us in Jesus to be free of the burden of sin. We hide our sin; we excuse it; we dilute its seriousness; we do anything but acknowledge our guilt. Yet it is the humble acknowledgment of our sin that leads us to freedom, that lifts the heavy burden from our backs and spirits, that sets us free to run the race, as Saint Paul calls us to do (see 1 Corinthians 9:24–27; Hebrews 12:1).

When we truly repent, we too can hear the Father's words to us, his beloved sons and daughters. United with Jesus and repenting of our sin, we can please our Father too.

Let us, day in and day out, fling off the burden of "sin which clings so closely" (Hebrews 12:1), that we might hear the voice of the Father and of his beloved Son in the Holy Spirit. Let us, through repentance, allow the scales to fall from our eyes and let our ears be unstopped, that we may be able to genuinely listen, to hear the plan of God and carry it out.

Behold!

The next day [John] saw Jesus coming toward him, and said,
"Behold, the Lamb of God, who takes away the sin of the
world! This is he of whom I said, 'After me comes a man
who ranks before me, for he was before me.' I myself did not
know him; but for this I came baptizing with water, that he
might be revealed to Israel." And John bore witness, "I saw
the Spirit descend as a dove from heaven and remain on
him. I myself did not know him; but he who sent me to bap-
tize with water said to me, 'He on whom you see the Spirit
descend and remain, this is he who baptizes with the Holy
Spirit.' And I have seen and have borne witness that this is
the Son of God."

(John 1:29–34)

TAKE A LOOK AT THE BEGINNING OF VERSE 31: "I MYSELF DID
not know him." John repeats this in verse 33. Yet John and
Jesus were cousins, and both were very holy men. John must
have loved Jesus very much, but John did not *know* that Jesus
was the Messiah!

John, like everyone else, must have had ideas about the
Messiah, specifically that he would free the Jewish people
from their enemies. For most people that was interpreted in
earthly terms. The Messiah would free them from the
Romans, the hated oppressors, free them from the taxes that
the Romans imposed, free them from poverty. Free, free,
free! But Jesus did not fit these notions that the Jewish people

held about the Messiah.

Now, John was a man who was obedient to God and to God's law. He prayed, he fasted, and he prepared himself for his mission. So when Christ was revealed in the Jordan, John was ready to hear and to obey, even though it turned his world upside down. He was able to recognize the voice of the Lord in his heart, in his spirit: "He on whom you see the Spirit of God descend and remain, this is the Messiah."

Can you imagine John's bewilderment in that moment? "This is my cousin," he might have thought. "I've known him all my life. He is a human being—a good, holy man—but he's a human, a man like me. I thought the Messiah would reveal himself in power and authority!" John must have stared, perhaps with his mouth hanging open.

Do you acknowledge Jesus as your Messiah? Are you following him closely? If God allows something to shatter all your preconceived notions about him, are you ready for that?

God's Word can reform us if we submit to its authority: "Thus says the Lord: Heaven is my throne and the earth is my footstool; what is the house which you would build for me, and what is the place of my rest? All these things my hand has made, so all these things are mine, says the Lord. But this is the man to whom I will look, he that is humble and contrite in spirit and trembles at my word" (Isaiah 66:1–2).

Can you hear God's voice? Do you know how to discern it from your own desires? And once you have discerned God's voice, are you ready to obey? Pope Benedict XVI said, "We cannot bring to the world the Good News which is Christ himself in person if we ourselves are not deeply united with Christ, if we do not know him profoundly, personally, if we do not live on his Words."[1]

FOLLOW ME

Now when he heard that John had been arrested, he withdrew into Galilee; and leaving Nazareth he went and dwelt in Capernaum by the sea, in the territory of Zebulun and Naphtali, that what was spoken by the prophet Isaiah might be fulfilled:

> "The land of Zebulun and the land of Naphtali,
> toward the sea, across the Jordan,
> Galilee of the Gentiles—
> the people who sat in darkness
> have seen a great light,
> and for those who sat in the region and shadow of
>   death
> light has dawned."

From that time Jesus began to preach, saying, "Repent, for the kingdom of heaven is at hand."

As he walked by the Sea of Galilee, he saw two brothers, Simon who is called Peter and Andrew his brother, casting a net into the sea; for they were fishermen. And he said to them, "Follow me, and I will make you fishers of men." Immediately they left their nets and followed him. And going on from there he saw two other brothers, James the son of Zebedee and John his brother, in the boat with Zebedee their father, mending their nets, and he called them. Immediately they left the boat and their father, and followed him.

And he went about all Galilee, teaching in their synagogues and preaching the gospel of the kingdom and healing every disease and every infirmity among the people.

(Matthew 4:12–23)

MATTHEW IS THE AUTHOR OF THIS GOSPEL. I IMAGINE THAT AS he wrote of Jesus' call of his friends, he must have thought of his own call. He was a hated tax collector, one who sided with the enemy. Yet when God called him, Matthew *immediately* left the relative security of a lucrative business to follow Jesus (see Matthew 9:9).

Now, in *this* passage, Matthew tells of Peter, Andrew, James and John doing the same thing. Notice the repetition of the word *immediately* (verses 20 and 22) in his description of their responses to Jesus' call. What was it about Jesus that made them able to so wholeheartedly and promptly respond?

If God spoke to your heart today and asked you to make a complete change—in your job, your living situation, who your friends are—could you do it? Have you spent enough time with the Lord to be attracted to him? Would you be able to hear his voice amid the noise and confusion and, yes, false priorities that the world offers?

Have you been evangelized by the world or by the Gospel? Pay attention to what you read, what you watch, what you listen to. There is a telling comparison between how much time you spend reading Scripture and how much time you spend watching TV. Some people I know have "fasted" from TV completely for a while, in order to honestly assess its effect on their lives.

Are you aware of the lyrics of the music you listen to and the effects they can have on your desires? We also need to consider our use of cell phones, the Internet, computer games, iPods and other electronics. We want to be totally wired to the Holy Spirit! He waits for open hearts and listening ears—and then he speaks.

God is a jealous God, and he will not compete with other interests. He calls today, loud and clear, just as he did in the time of the apostles and throughout history. "O that today you would listen to his voice! Harden not your hearts" (Psalm 95:7–8).

ARE YOU BLESSED?

Seeing the crowds, he went up on the mountain, and when he sat down his disciples came to him. And he opened his mouth and taught them, saying:

"Blessed are the poor in spirit, for theirs is the kingdom of heaven.

"Blessed are those who mourn, for they shall be comforted.

"Blessed are the meek, for they shall inherit the earth.

"Blessed are those who hunger and thirst for righteousness, for they shall be satisfied.

"Blessed are the merciful, for they shall obtain mercy.

"Blessed are the pure in heart, for they shall see God.

"Blessed are the peacemakers, for they shall be called sons of God.

"Blessed are those who are persecuted for righteousness' sake, for theirs is the kingdom of heaven.

"Blessed are you when men revile you and persecute you and utter all kinds of evil against you falsely on my account. Rejoice and be glad, for your reward is great in heaven, for so men persecuted the prophets who were before you."

(Matthew 5:1–12)

THIS IS THE WONDERFUL SERMON ON THE MOUNT. MATTHEW shows Jesus delivering these words to his disciples, those who were his closest followers. It is good for us to consider these words carefully, for we too are Jesus' followers. We want to be always close to his heart.

Here is another instance where Jesus turns our world upside down. Are we ready for this? Let's look at what Jesus is saying verse by verse.

Verse 3: Happy and blessed are those who consider God to be their greatest treasure. They spend their lives seeking to make him their portion. Is Jesus the highest priority of your life? Is he the center of your life, around whom everything else revolves?

Verse 4: Do you mourn over your sins? Over choices that implicitly make Jesus the second or third priority of your life? Do you mourn over the injustice in the world? Do you mourn over those who choose to serve other gods? Do you weep over those who have no one to preach the life-giving Word to them?

Verse 5: To be meek is to have our strength under control. Is your strength ruled by your love for God? Or do you resort to anger, bitterness and slander when you can't convince people of the truth or of your view of it? Do you depend on God to give you grace so that he can shine through in difficult, tense and stressful situations?

Even when you are genuinely in the right and defending *God's* truth, you must not resort to sinful means to try to convince others. Do you live by these principles? Do you trust God to help you when you are being attacked?

Verse 6: It is the food and drink of the blessed person to live righteously—that is, to live according to gospel teaching—and to defend others who seek to live righteously. Can you honestly say that righteous living is your nourishment? Or is it simply an elective appetizer, to be chosen only when it suits you?

Verse 7: Do you extend genuine mercy to those who have offended you? When they ask for forgiveness, do you forgive completely? Or do you recount their past mistakes over and over? Do you withhold forgiveness because you are angry and want your "pound of flesh"? Do you gossip, giving "your side" of the offense and speaking badly of others?

"As you did it to one of the least of these my brethren, you did it to me" (Matthew 25:40). If you are merciful, you will receive mercy when you stand before Jesus. Pretty great deal, if you ask me!

Verse 8: Do you guard your eyes, your ears, your mind, especially your memory, that they can be sentinels against the thief who seeks to destroy purity? What stand against the tide of filth have you taken in your own life and in your family? God is all pure; he is purity itself. You don't want anything in your life that would distance you from him in any way.

Verse 9: Blessed are those who can put aside their emotional reactions, prejudices and strong opinions to work for true peace, peace that is built on truth. Do you have the self-discipline to be a peacemaker? How can you work toward that?

Verses 10, 11 and 12: Blessed are those who stand for what is right, *who don't revile their persecutors* but simply stand for the truth, who refuse to back down, whatever the cost.

During the race riots of the 1960s here in the United States, a black Protestant pastor and his young family were experiencing persecution as people tried to force them from their neighborhood. Slogans were spray-painted on the house, other damage was done, warnings were given over the phone threatening their safety. It was a tense situation.

Police had given protection to the family, but one night a policeman finally said to the pastor, "Reverend, maybe you should move. I don't know if we can guarantee your safety. You have no idea how vicious these people can be."

The pastor, having prayed a great deal and consulted his wife, said to the police officer, "I know who I am, who we are. We are children of God, and God will protect us. These people just don't know that they are living next to royalty!"

Naïve? Not at all. That man's conviction that he was a son of God and that God would protect him in his time of trouble, that he served the King and was the King's heir, was deeply ingrained in him. His perseverance and that of his family won over the neighborhood. The family did not have to move, and the violence stopped. If the pastor perseveres in that kind of righteousness to the end of his life, his reward in heaven will be great. God is always faithful to his promises.

SALT AND LIGHT

"You are the salt of the earth; but if salt has lost its taste, how shall its saltiness be restored? It is no longer good for anything except to be thrown out and trodden under foot by men.

"You are the light of the world. A city set on a hill cannot be hidden. Nor do men light a lamp and put it under a bushel, but on a stand, and it gives light to all in the house. Let your light so shine before men, that they may see your good works and give glory to your Father who is in heaven."

(Matthew 5:13–16)

YOU AND I ARE CALLED TO BE SALT AND LIGHT. HOW CAN THIS happen?

First of all, it is essential to realize that Jesus means what he says. This is not just some poetic expression in his conversation with his disciples; we are to take it seriously. Jesus is asking us to express our discipleship in our conversations and our actions. We are to bring the presence of Christ into our families, our workplaces, our recreational gatherings and our parishes.

Are you salt? Salt seasons with truth and faith, with vision and encouragement, with prayer, with charity. Any of these "seasonings" sprinkled on painful, even seemingly hopeless situations can begin to change things.

Are you light? When we bring the light of hope, of perspective, of wisdom, of solidarity, that is, "standing with" others in times of suffering; when we bring mercy, kindness, a listening ear, we open the door to the Light—Jesus Christ. We are messengers, bearers of God's presence in the darkness.

I heard someone say that we are called to be the sanctuary lamp, signaling the presence of the Lord. That is another way of expressing God's call, through our baptism, to reflect him in every situation. The life of Christ was poured into us as we were cleansed of original sin. We became temples of the Holy Spirit (see 1 Corinthians 3:16–17). If we let the grace of God water our souls through prayer, the Eucharist and confession, we are empowered to live our destiny, to be light and salt to a darkened world and a tasteless culture.

A group of coworkers were running to catch a flight home. As they passed through the airport corridors, one of them accidentally hit a table that held a display of apples, scattering them on the floor. The men were already late, so most of them ran on.

But the last man in the group stopped, and he realized that the girl standing by the table was blind. Tears were rolling down her face as she tried to find the produce. The man yelled to his coworkers to call his wife and tell her he would be late. Then he began to pick up the apples, examining them and taking out the damaged ones. After doing a quick calculation, he put forty dollars into the girl's hand to cover the damaged apples. Then he reset her display.

Saying good-bye, he turned to go reschedule his flight. The girl called after him, "Sir, who are you? Jesus?"

That man was salt and light. What about you? Being salt and light doesn't always involve great and courageous acts; sometimes it means handling little inconveniences exceedingly well. We all can do that!

A High Calling

"Do not think that I have come to abolish the law and the prophets; I have come not to abolish them but to fulfil them. For truly, I say to you, till heaven and earth pass away, not an iota, not a dot, will pass from the law until all is accomplished. Whoever then relaxes one of the least of these commandments and teaches men so, shall be called least in the kingdom of heaven; but he who does them and teaches them shall be called great in the kingdom of heaven. For I tell you, unless your righteousness exceeds that of the scribes and Pharisees, you will never enter the kingdom of heaven.

"You have heard that it was said to the men of old, 'You shall not kill; and whoever kills shall be liable to judgment.' But I say to you that every one who is angry with his brother shall be liable to judgment; whoever insults his brother shall be liable to the council, and whoever says, 'You fool!' shall be liable to the hell of fire. So if you are offering your gift at the altar, and there remember that your brother has something against you, leave your gift there before the altar and go; first be reconciled to your brother, and then come and offer your gift. Make friends quickly with your accuser, while you are going with him to court, lest your accuser hand you over to the judge, and the judge to the guard, and you be put in prison; truly, I say to you, you will never get out till you have paid the last penny.

"You have heard that it was said, 'You shall not commit adultery.' But I say to you that every one who looks at a woman lustfully has already committed adultery with her in his heart. If your right eye causes you to sin, pluck it out and throw it away; it is better that you lose one of your members than that your whole body be thrown into hell. And if your right hand causes you to sin, cut it off and throw it away; it is better that you lose one of your members than that your whole body go into hell.

"It was also said, 'Whoever divorces his wife, let him give her a certificate of divorce.' But I say to you that every one who divorces his wife, except on the ground of unchastity, makes her an adulteress; and whoever marries a divorced woman commits adultery.

"Again you have heard that it was said to the men of old, 'You shall not swear falsely, but shall perform to the Lord what you have sworn.' But I say to you, Do not swear at all, either by heaven, for it is the throne of God, or by the earth, for it is his footstool, or by Jerusalem, for it is the city of the great King. And do not swear by your head, for you cannot make one hair white or black. Let what you say be simply 'Yes' or 'No'; anything more than this comes from the Evil One."

(Matthew 5:17–37)

WE ARE LOOKING HERE AT ONE OF THE CLEAREST PASSAGES IN Matthew about our conduct. The whole purpose of the commandments is to lead us into a relationship with the living God, whereby we can live in intimate union with him.

I often hear people say, "Neither the Church nor God can tell me what is right or wrong. I will figure it out for myself." There is a problem with such an attitude. Genuinely mature adults know that they don't "know it all." We are all human beings, affected by original sin and by our personal sin. We are wounded in such a way that, left to ourselves, our first thought is for our own advantage. We are self-focused, self-concerned.

When we recognize this about ourselves, we can turn around and begin to look to God; in other words, we can begin a process of conversion. We need to look to his wisdom and to truly wise human beings to help us break out of our self-focused cocoon. That's what puts us on the road to true maturity. We learn that if we follow God's Word, God's direction, God's way, peace comes into our hearts, a new kind of happiness. We find ourselves drawing closer in mind and heart to the Source of all goodness and truth and beauty. We begin to truly see the purpose for which we were created: to be united with our Creator in a happiness that no one can take from us.

Jesus' words in this passage from Matthew can bring us into true maturity. He shows us that the Law calls us to unselfishness, and as we follow that Law, we find Jesus himself. He is the fulfillment of the Law.

Jesus tells us not to dilute the call, not to pick and choose what we want to do. He wants us to bow our stubborn heads and ask God to help us, step by step, to do his full will, his way! I guarantee that if you do this, you will be happier and more at peace than you have ever been or imagined being.

I will not fool you: The path of conversion is hard. The flesh, the world and the devil will give you umpteen reasons to stay where you are. It hurts to give up habits that give you some satisfaction. It is difficult to leave behind unhealthy relationships. But God is worth the pain! Choose him, and you will receive a satisfaction that no one will take from you. For it is a satisfaction based not on the world's values but on the gospel. You will know genuine fulfillment in Christ!

The scribes and Pharisees did what was "right": They obeyed the Law. But they did this only to get people's admiration, the best places in the synagogues, the first places at table. They were doing the right things for the wrong reasons. That's why they would not enter the kingdom of heaven. In fact, Jesus called them whitened sepulchers, filled with dead men's bones (see Matthew 23:27). What an indictment!

Jesus always looks at the heart, at our motivation. When we make mistakes or when we fall—even disastrously—if we ask forgiveness and get up again, Jesus will love us even more and draw nearer to us. Think of the Good Shepherd who goes after that one lost sheep (see Luke 15:3–7).

In verses 21–22 Jesus ups the ante in the Christian walk: He asks his disciples to give up anger and hatred and revenge. He points out the fifth commandment but goes further in saying that there are many ways to kill. We can destroy others by violence in speech—by slander and calumny—and by rejection and exclusion.

Jesus never leaves us in our sin. In verses 23–26 he tells us how to right the relationships we have damaged. If we are going to Mass, to eucharistic adoration, to a prayer meeting, to a time of prayer within our family or by ourselves, and we realize that we have offended someone, Jesus says that we are to get up, leave that time of prayer, *go* to the person we have offended and ask forgiveness. Then we can go and pray. Even if we didn't intend the offense, and even if the other person is supersensitive, Jesus says that we are to resolve the relationship before coming to God in prayer.

Now, compare Matthew 5:23–24 with Matthew 18:15. Read carefully. *Note the initiative always rests with us!* Whether we offend or are offended, we are not off the hook. A high calling? A great demand? Yes! Ask the Holy Spirit for courage and wisdom. Keep leaning on him for help. He will not fail you.

Jesus also raises the issues of adultery and divorce. Often the parties in such cases are trying to justify their actions. The end result is never peace and resolution. Jesus tells us to be ruthless in dealing with our own sin *first.* Allow the spotlight of God's grace to pierce your heart—your motivations, your intentions. Be humbly honest with yourself; face your weakness or sin; face your very painful hurts and ask God to lead you as a true disciple in dealing with your failures.

God will draw near when we don't seek to excuse or minimize our part in very challenging relationships. If we follow God's will in humility, he will show us the way through the circumstances.

Finally, Jesus calls us to be men and women of integrity. Speak the truth simply and clearly, whatever the cost to you. Where you are right, say so; where you are wrong, acknowledge it. Jesus *is* the truth. When you stand and walk and speak in truth, he joins himself to you more closely.

God is very near to those who seek him. You will be surprised at the peace and assurance that come when you follow God's will.

LESSONS IN LOVE

"You have heard that it was said, 'An eye for an eye and a tooth for a tooth.' But I say to you, Do not resist one who is evil. But if any one strikes you on the right cheek, turn to him the other also; and if any one would sue you and take your coat, let him have your cloak as well; and if any one forces you to go one mile, go with him two miles. Give to him who begs from you, and do not refuse him who would borrow from you.

"You have heard that it was said, 'You shall love your neighbor and hate your enemy.' But I say to you, Love your enemies and pray for those who persecute you, so that you may be sons of your Father who is in heaven; for he makes his sun rise on the evil and on the good, and sends rain on the just and on the unjust. For if you love those who love you, what reward have you? Do not even the tax collectors do the same? And if you salute only your brethren, what more are you doing than others? Do not even the Gentiles do the same? You, therefore, must be perfect, as your heavenly Father is perfect."

(Matthew 5:38–48)

JESUS HERE ALLUDES TO AN OLD TESTAMENT MANDATE (SEE Exodus 21:24) that was meant to limit retributions for wrongdoing. It allowed punishments that were commensurate with the evil inflicted, so as to keep people from escalating violence. But, Jesus gives us a greater command that can stop the cycle of evil in its tracks: Rather than doing to your enemy what he has done to you, love him.

Jesus is not disposing of legitimate pursuits of justice in serious matters. A judge must penalize wrongdoers. A teacher must establish boundaries with her students, and penalties for wrongdoing are part of that process. An employer expects those who work for him to follow the standards he has established, and those who fail to meet his legitimate expectations should not be surprised to see a decrease in salary or loss of their job. These kinds of penalties are elements of a just and well-ordered society.

What Jesus is looking at is our heart, our motivation. He is speaking about our reactions to the selfishness, anger, hatred and bitterness that we experience. A Christian will *decide* not to further a wrongdoing by retaliation. He or she will seek to work out a problem by talking directly to the offending person—and only that person. On occasion we may need to seek advice in order to remedy a situation, but here we must be discerning. Is that a cloak to cover our desire to vent? Are we hoping to involve others in our defense? Gossip, calumny and slander are not the means of resolving wrongdoing.

The decision to "turn the other cheek" takes grace, and if we ask for grace, God will give it to us. He will give us the wisdom and strength to forget self and pursue peace—not peace at any price but peace based on charity and justice.

Is this hard? Of course it is. But God never commands without imparting power and the necessary gifts to carry out his Word. Our biggest problem is that we do not expect his help; we do not ask for it. We simply *react.*

We need self-control to *respond,* not react, to the painful words and actions of others. Ask God for this; it takes practice but yields the fruit of peace. We can become channels of peace through honest and frank discussion.

We must take our injuries to the heart of God and ask him to carry them, so they do not fester in us. Ask God for the courage to love the person who has offended you. Someday, maybe a year or two from now, the person may come to you and in some way express sorrow for the injury. If your heart has remained in prayer for the person and you have chosen to remain open to God's working through you, you will see fruit.

Having said all that and having seen the fruit of following God's Word in relationships, nevertheless I have to say that I still have one unresolved relationship in my life. I continue to pray for the other person, but I also pray for myself, that I may not yield to bitterness or hopelessness. Let us struggle together. God will not be outdone in generosity. He "richly furnishes us with everything to enjoy" (1 Timothy 6:18; see Luke 6:38).

Cardinal Christoph Schönborn wrote: "To love wherever we encounter love is nothing special. We find that easy. But to have goodwill toward the one who does us evil, this makes us like God, who is good to all whether they thank him or not. Moreover, history and our own experience show one thing: Revenge has never brought about peace. Somebody has to make the beginning of venturing the step toward the other person. And Jesus thinks that I should be that somebody."[1]

8

Do Not Be Anxious

"No one can serve two masters; for either he will hate the one and love the other, or he will be devoted to the one and despise the other. You cannot serve God and mammon.

"Therefore I tell you, do not be anxious about your life, what you shall eat or what you shall drink, nor about your body, what you shall put on. Is not life more than food, and the body more than clothing? Look at the birds of the air: they neither sow nor reap nor gather into barns, and yet your heavenly Father feeds them. Are you not of more value than they? And which of you by being anxious can add one cubit to his span of life? And why are you anxious about clothing? Consider the lilies of the field, how they grow; they neither toil nor spin; yet I tell you, even Solomon in all his glory was not clothed like one of these. But if God so clothes the grass of the field, which today is alive and tomorrow is thrown into the oven, will he not much more clothe you, O you of little faith? Therefore do not be anxious, saying, 'What shall we eat?' or 'What shall we drink?' or 'What shall we wear?' For the Gentiles seek all these things; and your heavenly Father knows that you need them all. But seek first his kingdom and his righteousness, and all these things shall be yours as well.

"Therefore do not be anxious about tomorrow, for tomorrow will be anxious for itself. Let the day's own trouble be sufficient for the day."

(Matthew 6:24–34)

MANY PEOPLE TRY TO SERVE GOD AND AT THE SAME TIME CATER to their own flesh and the world's agenda. Theirs is a very insecure and vulnerable position, like having one foot on the dock and one foot in the boat. Look at your life from this perspective. Are your two feet firmly planted in God's kingdom? What can you do if they're not?

I hope you decide to choose God and his kingdom. Then you will begin to experience the blessings he describes in this passage from the Gospel. Notice that he doesn't promise wealth but that our needs will be met. He uses examples from nature. If the Father cares so well for animals and plants, how much more should we be assured that our Father will care for us human beings!

In order to experience this care, Jesus tells us, we are to "seek first his kingdom and his righteousness." That is, we are to put our time and energy into *obeying the commandments, growing in virtue* and *repenting when we fail*. Then we will know God's love and provision.

Not long ago a small red-winged blackbird died after flying into our living room window. I looked at that tiny creature, and surprisingly, tears came to my eyes. I was sorrowful that anything had to die, but at the same time my tears came from the joy of realizing that God knew that particular bird had died. He knew and cared! How much more then, he tells us, does he know everything about us, and how much more will he care for us. We are his precious sons and daughters. "Trust me!" he says. "Follow me!"

9

Where Does Your House Stand?

"Not every one who says to me, 'Lord, Lord,' shall enter the kingdom of heaven, but he who does the will of my Father who is in heaven. On that day many will say to me, 'Lord, Lord, did we not prophesy in your name, and cast out demons in your name, and do many mighty works in your name?' And then will I declare to them, 'I never knew you; depart from me, you evildoers.'

"Every one then who hears these words of mine and does them will be like a wise man who built his house upon the rock; and the rain fell, and the floods came, and the winds blew and beat upon that house, but it did not fall, because it had been founded on the rock. And every one who hears these words of mine and does not do them will be like a foolish man who built his house upon the sand; and the rain fell, and the floods came, and the winds blew and beat against that house, and it fell; and great was the fall of it."

And when Jesus finished these sayings, the crowds were astonished at his teaching, for he taught them as one who had authority, and not as their scribes.

(Matthew 7:21–28)

THIS IS A HARD SET OF VERSES TO READ, AND THEY ARE VERSES that need to be pondered. A hasty reading means you may miss the message.

First the passage tells us that saying many prayers does not assure us of God's pleasure now or on Judgment Day. We can pray multitudinous words and have them count for nothing. We can even serve day in and day out the needs of others. We can be known for good works and gain nothing in the sight of God!

What pleases the Lord? What does count? He wants us to *hear* his words and *do* them.

I suggest you ask yourself some searching questions: Do I pray, love and serve in order to accomplish God's will, to be more and more conformed to his likeness? Or do I pray, love and serve in order that others will think well of me? Do I think that I accumulate "brownie points" by my prayers and service?

Let's be honest with ourselves. Our pride gets in the way—a lot! The tendency of our fallen human nature is to compete, to strive to get ahead, by good means or foul. We can bring that spirit of competition into spiritual matters as well. It's called hypocrisy, and it does not serve or please God.

God always looks at the heart, the intention, when we work and pray. We need to make sure that we are building our houses, that is, our lives, on the rock that is Christ. We must treasure his Word and his sacraments to be secure in Christ.

Several years ago in California there were some terrible storms. The rain water and the wind demolished many homes that were built on hillsides. Those homes had not been built with appropriate precautions. There was very little land surrounding them, so they had no secure foundation. Realtors sold the homes based on the view or on the celebrities the owners would encounter in the neighborhood. The owners allowed themselves to be dazzled by fancy promises.

Many of us act in a similar way with our lives, our immortal souls. We become dazzled by the world's promises and then consumed by them. To the extent that we allow that, we are building on sand. On the other hand, Jesus' Word, the commandments, the sacraments, the love and service we give to those in need—all with the right intentions—form the rock on which we can build with confidence.

Verse 28 says that everyone was "astonished" at Jesus' teaching. Why? Because his teaching came with conviction and with a great love for the Father. People heard it and were attracted. They saw goodness; they witnessed peace and confidence.

The scribes and the Pharisees knew the Law inside and out. Their observance of it was strict and sterile, not based on love but on a desire to be praised, to be thought well of. That is sand!

How solid is the foundation of your house? Are you talking the talk *and* walking the walk?

10

The Good Doctor

As Jesus passed on from there, he saw a man called Matthew sitting at the tax office; and he said to him, "Follow me." And he rose and followed him.

And as he sat at table in the house, behold, many tax collectors and sinners came and sat down with Jesus and his disciples. And when the Pharisees saw this, they said to his disciples, "Why does your teacher eat with tax collectors and sinners?" But when he heard it, he said, "Those who are well have no need of a physician, but those who are sick. Go and learn what this means, 'I desire mercy, and not sacrifice.' For I came not to call the righteous, but sinners."

(Matthew 9:9–13)

THE JEWS HATED THE TAX COLLECTOR. HE WAS A TRAITOR, serving the Roman government and taking from the people the little they had. Further, his means of collection were often unscrupulous and self-serving.

Matthew was one of these hated men, barely tolerated. But Jesus looked at him, saw something redeemable in his heart and called him. Matthew's response was immediate—a true testimony to something good in his heart.

Many others of questionable background, public sinners, felt drawn to this itinerant preacher. They came to Jesus and listened to him. And Jesus did not exclude them. Never had they been treated so lovingly.

The Pharisees, seeing the attention that the riffraff were paying Jesus, were indignant and jealous, and they challenged the disciples. Jesus heard this, and his reply to the Pharisees defines his mission: "I have come," he said in essence, "for the poor, the weak, the blind, the lame, the sinner." In other words, he comes for all those in need, spiritually, materially, physically.

He has come for you and me! He extends mercy and healing for our innumerable wounds. He is the good doctor. He is not expecting us to fix ourselves up and then present ourselves to him. So come to him with your diseases and wounds, spiritual and physical. "Come to me, all who labor and are heavy laden, and I will give you rest" (Matthew 11:28).

Many people today think that their sins and diseases are barriers to God, when in reality they are the ticket of admission. God says, "I desire mercy and not sacrifice." Jesus told the Pharisees that all their animal sacrifices were not pleasing to God because they did not have a heart of worship but rather tried to appease God with an external act.

God expects mercy to mark each follower of Christ. How can we extend that mercy if we have not humbled ourselves before God, if we have hidden our wounds? We can only give the mercy of God to others if we have first received it from his wounded heart. He wants us to offer our wounds to him for healing.

"God will not deny His mercy to anyone," wrote Saint Faustina. "Heaven and earth may change, but God's mercy will never be exhausted."[1]

May we lay down our pride the way Jesus hoped the Pharisees would. May we be unafraid about being in the company of sinners who seek mercy. Jesus will receive us with open arms! It is for this that he came.

11

WANTED: DISCIPLES!

When he saw the crowds, he had compassion for them, because they were harassed and helpless, like sheep without a shepherd. Then he said to his disciples, "The harvest is plentiful, but the laborers are few; pray therefore the Lord of the harvest to send out laborers into his harvest."

And he called to him his twelve disciples and gave them authority over unclean spirits, to cast them out, and to heal every disease and every infirmity. The names of the twelve apostles are these: first, Simon, who is called Peter, and Andrew his brother; James the son of Zebedee, and John his brother; Philip and Bartholomew; Thomas and Matthew the tax collector; James the son of Alphaeus, and Thaddaeus; Simon the Cananaean, and Judas Iscariot, who betrayed him.

These Twelve Jesus sent out, charging them, "Go nowhere among the Gentiles, and enter no town of the Samaritans, but go rather to the lost sheep of the house of Israel. And preach as you go, saying, 'The kingdom of heaven is at hand.' Heal the sick, raise the dead, cleanse lepers, cast out demons. You received without pay, give without pay."

(Matthew 9:36—10:8)

SHEEP WITHOUT A SHEPHERD ARE PITIFUL! THEY CAN STRAY, moving into other owners' fields because the grass looks greener over there. They can become cast—that is, they stumble, fall, can't get up and may actually die if no one helps them within a few hours. They can fight among themselves and injure one another. Wolves can attack the vulnerable ones.

All of these situations have their human counterparts. Humans too can stray from their Shepherd—"I don't need help; I don't need God"—only to find that they are far from him when they do need help. They are prone to selfishness and pride, which often lead to damaged relationships, isolation from others and subjection to the world's lies.

Jesus looked on the crowd and had compassion. What did he see? Certainly he saw those who have just been described. He saw all the sin and wounds and pain that humans inflict on themselves and on one another. And he grieved for that.

Jesus knows what direction and healing and deliverance his people need. He knows what is possible if we turn to him in our weakness and fear and anger. But he also cries out to the Father for more laborers, for more men and women who would help him in shepherding his people.

We should pray for more priests. We should ask the Father for good and holy men who will step forward and sacrifice their lives for the salvation of others. And we should pray that men and women in every walk of life will step forward and generously do their part to help people come into a place of safety and security in Christ.

Jesus told his disciples to preach that the kingdom of heaven was at hand. He meant that the Messiah had come. Those people could reach out and touch the kingdom by putting their faith in Jesus. Yet many of the people of that time heard his teaching and turned away. They missed the justice and peace and joy that come from being a disciple, a follower of Jesus.

If we follow Jesus closely and put our faith in him, we will experience the fruit. God will give us some share in bringing the gospel to the deaf and the blind and the suffering. He will give us the power to heal—sometimes physically, always spiritually.

Some years ago I was on a mission trip in Eastern Europe with a team of about twenty people. We preached and ministered to large numbers of individuals who had been worn down by years under communism. They had been deprived of the sacraments and robbed of their faith. Many were weary to the bone with daily struggles.

One of the men on our team was suffering from multiple sclerosis (MS). His wife was also ill, but in prayer they both had thought that the man should go on this mission trip. During a break in the conference, this man walked off the stage to get a glass of water. He was stopped by a woman who had her seven-year-old granddaughter with her, a child blind from birth. "Will you pray with her? Will you ask Jesus to heal her eyes?"

"Of course I will ask Jesus," this man thought. He laid his hands on the child's eyes briefly and asked Jesus to make her better. Then he left to get his glass of water.

When the man came back into the conference room, what did he see but this woman standing on the stage with her little granddaughter, announcing through our translators that the girl could see! A few moments later the family's pastor approached the stage and testified that the little girl had indeed been blind since birth. God used a man with MS who was willing to serve; despite his own weakness God used him to bring healing to someone else!

God needs humble disciples of faith to reach the lost sheep. Will you step forward? Will you look beyond your own weaknesses and obstacles to let God work through you?

It will not be easy; the pathway is in and through the cross. But for all eternity the Lord himself will bless you and thank you. You will experience union with all Truth, all Beauty, all Goodness forever!

Say yes to being his disciple. Commit yourself anew to be faithful to his Word. The Shepherd has need of you.

Every good thing in you and from you is a gift from God. Give it away with no strings attached. What you have received, give as a gift.

12

FEAR NOT!

"So have no fear of them; for nothing is covered that will not be revealed, or hidden that will not be known. What I tell you in the dark, utter in the light; and what you hear whispered, proclaim upon the housetops. And do not fear those who kill the body but cannot kill the soul; rather fear him who can destroy both soul and body in hell. Are not two sparrows sold for a penny? And not one of them will fall to the ground without your Father's will. But even the hairs of your head are all numbered. Fear not, therefore; you are of more value than many sparrows. So every one who acknowledges me before men, I also will acknowledge before my Father who is in heaven; but whoever denies me before men, I also will deny before my Father who is in heaven."

(Matthew 10:26–33)

THE "THEM" OF WHOM JESUS IS SPEAKING IN THE FIRST VERSE are those who persecute Christians. Don't fear them, Jesus tells us. They have no power to destroy our souls, no power to take away our eternal inheritance—unless of course we allow them to do that by succumbing to hatred and revenge.

Francis Xavier Nguyen Van Thuan knew the truth of these words. This Vietnamese cardinal endured years of captivity, many of them in solitary confinement. One night he was overwhelmed by the sin and darkness and isolation. A thought came to him: "Francis, you are still very rich. You have the love of Christ in your heart. Love them as Jesus has loved you." The cardinal set about doing just that with his prison guards, and out of the fire of suffering in his learning to love came pure gold! "Jesus has taught me to love you," he told his astonished guards, "if I do not, I am no longer worthy of being called a Christian."[1]

God is offering you the grace that Cardinal Van Thuan had. Will you accept it?

The only one to fear is the devil, "who can destroy both soul and body in hell," and even he cannot destroy you unless you allow yourself to be seduced by evil. Many people flirt with this disastrous possibility by dabbling in drugs and alcohol and illicit sex. To what do you turn when you are under severe stress?

Come to Jesus. He will show you the way. He knows every single little physical characteristic of yours; he intimately knows your virtues and vices, your hopes and dreams, your pain and suffering. He also loves you and desires to care for you, not only in the big things but in the little details.

If you turn to Jesus, ask pardon when you fail and let him truly reign as the Savior of your life, the day will come when he will escort you before the whole heavenly kingdom and acknowledge that you belong to him. The Father will look at you and see the image of his Son in you! He will say, "Well done, good and faithful servant.... Enter into the joy of your master!" (Matthew 25:21, 23). Can you imagine the glory of that day?

That is real; it is a greater reality than everything around us right now. These things will pass away, but the kingdom and its relationships will last *forever.*

13

Worth the Cost

"He who loves father or mother more than me is not worthy of me; and he who loves son or daughter more than me is not worthy of me; and he who does not take his cross and follow me is not worthy of me. He who finds his life will lose it, and he who loses his life for my sake will find it.

"He who receives you receives me, and he who receives me receives him who sent me. He who receives a prophet because he is a prophet shall receive a prophet's reward, and he who receives a righteous man because he is a righteous man shall receive a righteous man's reward. And whoever gives to one of these little ones even a cup of cold water because he is a disciple, truly, I say to you, he shall not lose his reward."

(Matthew 10:37–42)

IN THE FIRST VERSE HERE, JESUS SPELLS OUT THE COST OF being a disciple in stark, uncompromising terms. Practically, his words mean that if people are asking you to do things contrary to God's commandments, contrary to the gospel, then to be a true disciple you need to say no to them. The true disciple chooses Christ and his way over the requests or even demands of family members and friends.

Does something die in you when you have to make that choice or when you consider making it? It is hard to be a disciple: It requires faith; it requires hope in God's promises. Sometimes we have to make choices that feel like falling from some precipice. Yes, discipleship costs, but being faithful to the Lord will bring blessings that we can't yet see.

Some time ago a woman called me with an all-too-familiar story. Her adult daughters had at different times asked if they could use the family vacation home. The response was always yes, until the parents found out that the daughters were bringing male friends to share the vacation home and its beds. This realization brought the parents great sorrow.

The mother told her daughters, "I cannot allow you to come and live that way in the home that belongs to this family."

The daughters' response: "Well, you are no longer our mother."

Painful? Yes, to that mother it was like death! She "lost" her life in this encounter, having to go against her mother's heart, but in choosing the Lord and his way over even this most intimate of relationships, God will bless her. And her discipleship affords her daughters a grace to move toward new life, if they will receive and heed her counsel.

This is what Jesus means when he says, "He who loses his life for my sake will find it." The gospel is full of similar paradoxes: The one who dies will live; the one who gives will have more; the one who sells all will find the greatest of all treasures: Jesus. (See, for example, John 12:24–25; Mark 4:24; 10:29–30; Matthew 13:47.)

But it takes faith, doesn't it? We have to *believe* that Jesus is true to his promises, that if we live fully for him in whatever state of life to which he has called us, he will give himself fully to us in ways that will lead us to eternal union with him.

Here again, God's Word is our surety. We know that "he spoke, and it came to be; he commanded, and it stood forth" (Psalm 33:9). Let's not hold back but put all our trust in him. "The sufferings of the present time are not worth comparing with the glory that is to be revealed to us" (Romans 8:18).

14

Yoked With Jesus

At that time Jesus declared, "I thank you, Father, Lord of heaven and earth, that you have hidden these things from the wise and understanding and revealed them to infants; yes, Father, for such was your gracious will. All things have been delivered to me by my Father; and no one knows the Son except the Father, and no one knows the Father except the Son and any one to whom the Son chooses to reveal him. Come to me, all who labor and are heavy laden, and I will give you rest. Take my yoke upon you, and learn from me; for I am gentle and lowly in heart, and you will find rest for your souls. For my yoke is easy, and my burden is light."

(Matthew 11:25–30)

GOD LOVES TO REVEAL THINGS TO CHILDREN, JESUS SAYS. Perhaps that is because they are more open to receiving what he has to show.

I remember one day, when I was a very little girl, trying to carry a bag of groceries into the house. I pushed, pulled, kicked and shoved, but I could not do it. And because I was stubborn and didn't want to say that I could not do it, I would not ask for help.

My dad watched this for a few minutes and then came up behind me. Whispering in my ear not to turn around, he told me to grab the top of the bag from behind. I did, then I lifted it, and the bag was light. I carried the bag into the house on my back, thrilled that I *could* do it.

Then Dad showed me that he was holding the bag from the bottom. "Daddies are here to help until you grow big and strong. Daddies love to help. Ask me. It will make me happy." My four-year-old mind understood, and I let go of my pride (at least in that instance!).

As an adult, I have to return to the simplicity of what I learned as a child. Pride is deep, and I find myself still going headlong into some issue or project "on my own steam," forgetting to ask for help until I meet failure and don't know what to do. I have to learn again to ask my heavenly Father each time I am in need.

It helps at those times to recall what my beloved earthly father taught me: to turn to my Father in heaven with simplicity and humility. The burden becomes easier because I am not alone; the yoke becomes easier because I am yoked *with his Son*. Jesus is not standing on the sidelines cheering me on. He is with me, beside me at every moment. Though the cross is heavy, we are carrying it together, and he is definitely carrying most of the weight!

What burdens are you carrying today? Is money running short? Is there conflict in your family? Are you or a loved one battling illness?

God loves you! He is with you, right in the midst of your struggles. So pocket your pride and open your hands, asking for his help.

15

Good Souls, Good Soil

That same day Jesus went out of the house and sat beside the sea. And great crowds gathered about him, so that he got into a boat and sat there; and the whole crowd stood on the beach. And he told them many things in parables, saying: "A sower went out to sow. And as he sowed, some seeds fell along the path, and the birds came and devoured them. Other seeds fell on rocky ground, where they had not much soil, and immediately they sprang up, since they had no depth of soil, but when the sun rose they were scorched; and since they had no root they withered away. Other seeds fell upon thorns, and the thorns grew up and choked them. Other seeds fell on good soil and brought forth grain, some a hundredfold, some sixty, some thirty. He who has ears, let him hear."

Then the disciples came and said to him, "Why do you speak to them in parables?" And he answered them, "To you it has been given to know the secrets of the kingdom of heaven, but to them it has not been given. For to him who has will more be given, and he will have abundance; but from him who has not, even what he has will be taken away. This is why I speak to them in parables, because seeing they do not see, and hearing they do not hear, nor do they under-stand. With them indeed is fulfilled the prophecy of Isaiah which says:

'You shall indeed hear but never understand,
   and you shall indeed see but never perceive.
For this people's heart has grown dull,
   and their ears are heavy of hearing,
   and their eyes they have closed,
lest they should perceive with their eyes,
   and hear with their ears,
and understand with their heart,
   and turn for me to heal them.'

But blessed are your eyes, for they see, and your ears, for they hear. Truly, I say to you, many prophets and righteous men longed to see what you see, and did not see it, and to hear what you hear, and did not hear it.

"Hear then the parable of the sower. When any one hears the word of the kingdom and does not understand it, the Evil One comes and snatches away what is sown in his heart; this is what was sown along the path. As for what was sown on rocky ground, this is he who hears the word and immediately receives it with joy; yet he has no root in himself, but endures for a while, and when tribulation or persecution arises on account of the word, immediately he falls away. As for what was sown among thorns, this is he who hears the word, but the cares of the world and the delight in riches choke the word, and it proves unfruitful. As for what was sown on good soil, this is he who hears the word and understands it; he indeed bears fruit, and yields, in one case a hundredfold, in another sixty, and in another thirty."

(Matthew 13:1–23)

I THINK WE WOULD ALL SAY THAT THE LESSON HERE IS CLEAR, because Jesus himself explains the fate of the different seeds. But it is the application to ourselves that is of paramount importance to our walk in the Christian life. Here are some questions to consider in this regard:

1. Do you rely on the grace of baptism to water your soul? I have found it good to ask God almost daily, "Renew in me today the graces of my baptism. Help me to remember that, before any other identity, I am your daughter. Help me to live today in accord with that fundamental reality and identity."

A friend told me that when he applied for a passport renewal, he wished he could claim himself a citizen of heaven before declaring himself a citizen of the United States. "I want to keep reminding myself," he said, "of my fundamental identity and where I'm headed."

2. When you encounter something you don't understand, do you seek the truth? Do you look for good reading materials? Do you study the Bible?

3. Do you resist the temptation to live merely for the day, to seek "fun" twenty-four/seven? Are you a good steward of your body and soul, knowing that the day will come when you will have to render an account?

4. Do you find conferences, retreats and parish missions stimulating for your soul? Do the joy and peace you experience there last more than a day or two, or do you let daily concerns crowd back in? Do new interests clamor for attention, making it hard for you to remember what the retreat was all about, what you promised God and yourself?

Life can go on after a spiritual encounter with little or no change. If this is the case for you, it may be hard for you to endure difficult times, because the seed of his Word and his grace will have withered. Examine yourself. What have you done with the graces and favors you have received? Don't treat God's gifts lightly!

5. What chokes the blessings of God's Word in you? What chokes the harvest of thirty, sixty, a hundredfold? Do the cares of this world burden you? Seek God's sustaining help. Do the pleasures of this world distract you? Seek the delights of God's presence.

6. "Your word is a lamp to my feet and a light to my path" (Psalm 119:105). Do you experience that as true? If not, why not? How can you allow God's Word to genuinely nourish your spirit and help you love him and others more? Have you asked God for help with this?

16

Kingdom Growth

Another parable he put before them, saying, "The kingdom of heaven may be compared to a man who sowed good seed in his field; but while men were sleeping, his enemy came and sowed weeds among the wheat, and went away. So when the plants came up and bore grain, then the weeds appeared also. And the servants of the householder came and said to him, 'Sir, did you not sow good seed in your field? How then has it weeds?' He said to them, 'An enemy has done this.' The servants said to him, 'Then do you want us to go and gather them?' But he said, 'No; lest in gathering the weeds you root up the wheat along with them. Let both grow together until the harvest; and at harvest time I will tell the reapers, Gather the weeds first and bind them in bundles to be burned, but gather the wheat into my barn.'"

Another parable he put before them, saying, "The kingdom of heaven is like a grain of mustard seed which a man took and sowed in his field; it is the smallest of all seeds, but when it has grown it is the greatest of shrubs and becomes a tree, so that the birds of the air come and make nests in its branches."

He told them another parable. "The kingdom of heaven is like leaven which a woman took and hid in three measures of flour, till it was all leavened."

All this Jesus said to the crowds in parables; indeed he said nothing to them without a parable. This was to fulfil what was spoken by the prophet:

"I will open my mouth in parables,

I will utter what has been hidden since the foundation of the world."

Then he left the crowds and went into the house. And his disciples came to him, saying, "Explain to us the parable of the weeds of the field." He answered, "He who sows the good seed is the Son of man; the field is the world, and the good seed means the sons of the kingdom; the weeds are the sons of the evil one, and the enemy who sowed them is the devil; the harvest is the close of the age, and the reapers are angels. Just as the weeds are gathered and burned with fire, so will it be at the close of the age. The Son of man will send his angels, and they will gather out of his kingdom all causes of sin and all evildoers, and throw them into the furnace of fire, where there will be weeping and gnashing of teeth. Then the righteous will shine like the sun in the kingdom of their Father. He who has ears, let him hear."

(Matthew 13:24–43)

CAREFULLY READ THE FIRST PARABLE HERE. IT SHOWS US clearly that the good and the bad, the pure of heart and the evil (and the mediocre), will grow up side by side: same family, same office, same parish. The "weeds" will remain until the harvest. We can grow stronger by rejecting their enticements and by planting seeds of charity and kindness and hope. We can crowd out the evil around us and diminish its effects.

Years ago I taught a class of academically challenged

teenagers. Most of the forty-two students were boys. Many had poor hygiene, and manners were nonexistent. My first reactions were hopelessness and anger. But I began to pray and watch and listen. I also did a little homework of my own.

I learned that one boy was raising a younger brother and sister at home, virtually alone. One had lived in a home where a relative had been murdered and the body locked in a closet. One had lost a father to suicide. And on it went. This was the 1960s and 1970s, middle-class America, a Catholic school.

Even my extensive education had not prepared me to deal with the tragic effects of such circumstances. As I prayed and watched and listened, I decided that my first and most important task was to give these young people a safe haven for whatever hours of the day they spent with me. I stocked the top drawer of my desk with toothbrushes, soap, deodorant, shampoo and other items. When one boy finally had the courage to admit that he didn't know how to shave or use deodorant, I found someone to help him. Little victories like that one began to happen.

Then one day I noticed that the students were starting to listen when I spoke. Some would tell others to be quiet so I could be heard. They started to ask questions, and they began to learn!

The biggest victory came at the end of a long day, as I was sitting at my desk correcting papers. Three or four students came in and asked if they could sit in my room to do homework, talk and relax. (That's the day I learned how to toss a wad of paper from my desk into the waste can in the back of the room.) Some months later a student told me, "I feel safe here." Another said, "I can think here." And another, "I just like being in this room; it's warm and happy." I knew what they meant.

So when I think of a field of weeds and wheat growing up together, my first thought is not to destroy the weeds but to increase the wheat, the flowers, the good things. The good has power to overcome the evil within us as well as next to us. Try it in your own circumstances. It takes patience, but when you cooperate with God, he can make all things new!

The next two parables tell us that the kingdom of heaven does not attract all the fanfare of the kingdom of this world. In fact, the examples Jesus use show that his approach is opposite to that of the world. Jesus speaks of a mustard seed and of yeast, both very small and even invisible once they are sub-merged in the garden or the dough. We can miss the kingdom and its work at first. We can miss the greatness of God's work in our hearts, because we expect something good to make headlines.

Learn to think as a son or daughter of the kingdom of God. Some of the most powerful works of God were done in silence: the Annunciation, the Incarnation and the call of the apostles, for example. God spoke to the prophet Elijah in "a still small voice" (1 Kings 19:12). "Be still," God says, "and know that I am God" (Psalm 46:10).

The manager of a local supermarket, in an effort to increase sales, advised his employees to personalize his or her service. No one did much about that suggestion, except for a young man with Down's syndrome who worked as a bagger. With the help of his father, he made hundreds of business-size cards with inspirational thoughts. He dropped a card in each order of groceries he bagged.

Two weeks later the manager noticed that "John's line"

stretched clear down the aisle to the frozen foods. The manager opened another register and welcomed people to his line. No one moved. Puzzled, the manager asked individual customers to come to his open line. "No," they replied, "we want John's cards."

Sales in the store increased significantly. Other workers were inspired. The flower department decided to give away flowers at the end of the day to the elderly, widows and children.

We can build the kingdom by small, steady acts of kindness. I suggest you read the lives of Thérèse of Lisieux and Father Solanus Casey to see how possible it is to achieve holiness through the little things—holiness that will change others' lives and not just our own. Heaven will be a marvelous surprise, when we see whom God features, who makes the headlines.

God will work with your personality, but make sure that you are attentive to his direction. Learn to listen, to be still and wait; this is essential for a disciple. As the final verse of this Gospel passage tells us, let those ears of yours hear the voice of the Holy Spirit!

"This is the way, walk in it" (Isaiah 30:21). God is very near to you, and he wants to direct you—sometimes through inspiration, sometimes through a good pastor or a good friend, sometimes through a good book and always through his Word!

17

THE GREATEST TREASURE

"The kingdom of heaven is like treasure hidden in a field, which a man found and covered up; then in his joy he goes and sells all that he has and buys that field.

"Again, the kingdom of heaven is like a merchant in search of fine pearls, who, on finding one pearl of great value, went and sold all that he had and bought it.

"Again, the kingdom of heaven is like a net which was thrown into the sea and gathered fish of every kind; when it was full, men drew it ashore and sat down and sorted the good into vessels but threw away the bad. So it will be at the close of the age. The angels will come out and separate the evil from the righteous, and throw them into the furnace of fire, where there will be weeping and gnashing of teeth.

"Have you understood all this?" They said to him, "Yes." And he said to them, "Therefore every scribe who has been trained for the kingdom of heaven is like a householder who brings out of his treasure what is new and what is old."

(Matthew 13:44–52)

WHAT IS THE TREASURE HIDDEN IN THE FIELD? WHAT IS THE pearl of great price? Your relationship with Jesus Christ. Everything you were created for, everything you seek and long for, is answered in him. Do you believe that?

The apostle John put it this way:

That which was from the beginning, which we have heard, which we have seen with our eyes, which we have looked upon and touched with our hands, concerning the word of life—the life was made manifest, and we saw it, and testify to it, and proclaim to you the eternal life which was with the Father and was made manifest to us—that which we have seen and heard we proclaim also to you, so that you may have fellowship with us; and our fellowship is with the Father and with his Son Jesus Christ.

(1 John 1:1–3)

How highly do you value this relationship? What are you willing to yield, let go of, turn away from, in order to know more intimately Jesus Christ, your Lord and Savior? Pope Benedict said at the beginning of his pontificate: "If we let Christ into our lives, we lose nothing, nothing, absolutely nothing of what makes life free, beautiful and great."[1]

Don't let the world deceive you. Put this relationship first in your life, and other things will fall into their rightful place.

Another beloved pope of our time, John Paul II, encouraged us to take advantage of the storehouse of the Church's teaching, both the old and the new:

The great mystical tradition of the Church of both East and West…shows how prayer can progress, as a genuine dialogue of love, to the point of rendering the person wholly possessed by the divine Beloved, vibrating at the Spirit's touch, resting filially within the Father's heart. This is the lived experience of Christ's promise: "He who loves me will be loved by my Father, and I will love him and manifest myself to him" (Jn 14:21). It is a journey totally sustained by grace, which nonetheless demands an intense spiritual commitment and is no stranger to painful purifications.... But it leads, in various possible ways, to the ineffable joy experienced by the mystics as "nuptial union." How can we forget here, among the many shining examples, the teachings of St. John of the Cross and St. Teresa of Avila?

Yes, dear brothers and sisters, our Christian communities must become *genuine "schools" of prayer,* where the meeting with Christ is expressed not just in imploring help, but also in thanksgiving, praise, adoration, contemplation, listening, and ardent devotion until the heart truly "falls in love." Intense prayer, yes, but it does not distract us from our commitment to history: by opening our heart to the love of God it also opens it to the love of our brothers and sisters, and makes us capable of shaping history according to God's plan.[2]

18

BREAD, FISH AND MILK

Now when Jesus heard this, he withdrew from there in a boat to a lonely place apart. But when the crowds heard it, they followed him on foot from the towns. As he went ashore he saw a great throng; and he had compassion on them, and healed their sick. When it was evening, the disciples came to him and said, "This is a lonely place, and the day is now over; send the crowds away to go into the villages and buy food for themselves." Jesus said, "They need not go away; you give them something to eat." They said to him, "We have only five loaves here and two fish." And he said, "Bring them here to me." Then he ordered the crowds to sit down on the grass; and taking the five loaves and the two fish he looked up to heaven, and blessed, and broke and gave the loaves to the disciples, and the disciples gave them to the crowds. And they all ate and were satisfied. And they took up twelve baskets full of the broken pieces left over. And those who ate were about five thousand men, besides women and children.

(Matthew 14:13–21)

VERSE 13 SAYS, "NOW WHEN JESUS HEARD THIS…" "WHAT DID Jesus hear?" I asked myself. Once again we look at the verses right before these so that we have the proper context. The first part of chapter fourteen shows Jesus receiving the news of the beheading of John the Baptist. How sorrowful his heart must have been: John was a good, holy man and Jesus' relative.

So it makes perfect sense that Jesus seeks some time alone to pray to his Father. He tries! How many times have you been interrupted when you needed time alone? Jesus is not interrupted by just one person but by crowds, a great throng! What would you do?

I would be tempted to hide, to run away, reasoning that I owe myself this time alone (and sometimes we do). But Jesus gives us a powerful example of the selfless servant. Instead of being irritated, his heart is open to the crowds, and he heals their sick. Can you imagine the time and energy that took—hearing their needs, ministering to them? You might say, "Well, he was God, so it didn't cost him anything." But Jesus was incarnate, like us in all things but sin. He knew weariness (remember, he could sleep in a boat through a storm—Matthew 8:24); he knew loneliness and rejection, both of which weaken and drain us.

Then, right in the midst of serving, another need becomes evident: There is no food. Thousands of people, and not a store in sight! The disciples tell Jesus, "Let's bring this healing service to an end; send them away so they can find food."

Jesus has been giving evidence of his compassionate heart, and still the disciples don't "get it." So Jesus challenges them, "You give them something to eat." Immediately the disciples look around and conclude that this is impossible! "We have only five loaves and two fish." That is like having access to only five slices of pizza and two bags of popcorn at a high school football game. An utterly impossible situation!

But Jesus says, "Bring to me what you have." Can you imagine the disciples' looks and their thoughts? "Is this man crazy?" But they do what Jesus asks.

Then Jesus blesses the food and gives it *to the disciples* to distribute. What would you have done with that bread? Would you have walked out into the throng with it, or would you have run, afraid of the riot to come? Would you have been angry that you were asked to accomplish an impossible task?

Take some time right now and answer these questions. Be honest. Your responses will say some important things about your level of faith. Thank the Lord for the faith you have, and then ask him for more.

Imagine what went through the disciples' minds as they walked through that enormous crowd and saw that the little they had did not run out. They must have looked back at Jesus frequently with growing awe. I wonder if he didn't smile at them and urge them by his look to keep going.

Here Christ gives us two very powerful examples of his merciful heart: He heals, and he feeds everyone! Ask God to give you this heart, that the needs of others may become more important than your own.

Father Rick Thomas, a Jesuit priest and a good friend who has gone to be with the Lord, worked with the very poor in Juarez, Mexico. One day he received a shipment of food from the United States. It included some half pints of milk— something the children of the area needed badly. But when Father Rick counted the milk and counted the children before him, he realized that the milk supply was significantly short. He looked at the faces of the eager children and then turned to the Lord, asking his blessing.

With trepidation Father Rick began to distribute the milk. He purposely avoided looking in the box, instead reaching in for the next carton and asking God to feed his poor ones. When the last child had received milk, the box was empty. Father Rick knew that God had worked a miracle. He started to laugh and sing and bless God for his goodness.

Over the years that Father Rick worked with the poor, the multiplication of food happened again and again—always quietly, with no thunderclaps or trumpet blasts. Only those who had committed their lives to serve the poor and those with whom they shared the miracles knew about them! I was blessed to be one of the latter. And I know this story is true because I see in it the fingerprints of a faithful, merciful God.

That mercy continues today. Unite your heart with God!

19

Call on the Savior

Then he made the disciples get into the boat and go before him to the other side, while he dismissed the crowds. And after he had dismissed the crowds, he went up into the hills by himself to pray. When evening came, he was there alone, but the boat by this time was many furlongs distant from the land, beaten by the waves; for the wind was against them. And in the fourth watch of the night he came to them, walking on the sea. But when the disciples saw him walking on the sea, they were terrified, saying, "It is a ghost!" And they cried out for fear. But immediately he spoke to them, saying, "Take heart, it is I; have no fear."

And Peter answered him, "Lord, if it is you, bid me come to you on the water." He said, "Come." So Peter got out of the boat and walked on the water and came to Jesus; but when he saw the wind, he was afraid, and beginning to sink he cried out, "Lord, save me." Jesus immediately reached out his hand and caught him, saying to him, "O you of little faith, why did you doubt?" And when they got into the boat, the wind ceased. And those in the boat worshiped him, saying, "Truly you are the Son of God."

(Matthew 14:22–33)

THE DISCIPLES HAVE BEEN SERVING THE CROWDS FOR A WHILE, distributing the blessed bread and no doubt talking to them about Jesus. Remember that there were thousands of people on the hillside that day. The disciples are probably very tired. Jesus tells them to take the boat and go back to the other side of the lake.

The disciples battle the winds on the lake for many hours. Note that Jesus waits until the fourth watch, the last of the night watches, before coming to them. That time of night must have seemed very dark for the disciples, as things seem for us when we are grappling with difficult things, carrying heavy crosses. It is the time when we are most vulnerable, most prone to helplessness and hopelessness.

Then we realize that we can't make it alone. *This is the time Jesus chooses to reveal himself to us, just as he does here for his frightened disciples.* "Take heart, it is I; have no fear." We need to "hang on." Jesus is not playing games with us. He is allowing our faith to be tested, that we might grow in strength and become even more faith-filled disciples.

At first the disciples don't recognize Jesus. They think that they are seeing a ghost, which only adds to their terror. Then, right in the midst of their fear, they hear Jesus' voice. That is a miracle right there, given the noise of the wind and waves. They hear him say: "Take heart, it is I; have no fear."

Can you imagine what the disciples were thinking? "How can I not be afraid? We're about to drown; we're about to die!"

Once again Peter steps out in a certain level of faith. He basically says, "If it is you, prove it. Let me come to you." Peter knows that he has nothing to fear if it is Jesus walking toward them. Then he hears Jesus say, "Come!" And Peter, trusting Jesus, walks out on the water!

But instead of keeping his eyes on Jesus, Peter looks down, and his eyes fix on the circumstances: the howling wind, the high waves, the noise and confusion. Then he cries out the prayer of all of us: "Lord, save me!" Jesus reaches out, takes Peter's hand and says to him, "O you of little faith, why did you doubt?"

This is a question each of us needs to answer. We need to learn where our faith is weak. We need to strengthen our faith now, so that when the inevitable storms come, we are better prepared to trust and to keep our eyes fixed on Jesus. Saint Augustine said it well: "It is when things are peaceful that people should harvest the word of God for themselves, and store it in the inner recesses of their hearts, as the ant stores the results of summer's labor in the cavities of its nest. There is time to do this in the summer months, but winter will overtake us—the time of trouble, I mean—and unless we can find resources within ourselves we shall inevitably starve to death."[1]

Perhaps you are in turmoil now. Look for Jesus; listen for his voice among the many other voices that clamor for your attention. He will not fail to speak when you call on him from the pounding waves.

20

. . .

GREAT FAITH

And Jesus went away from there and withdrew to the district of Tyre and Sidon. And behold, a Canaanite woman from that region came out and cried, "Have mercy on me, O Lord, Son of David; my daughter is severely possessed by a demon." But he did not answer her a word. And his disciples came and begged him, saying, "Send her away, for she is crying after us." He answered, "I was sent only to the lost sheep of the house of Israel." But she came and knelt before him, saying, "Lord, help me." And he answered, "It is not fair to take the children's bread and throw it to the dogs." She said, "Yes, Lord, yet even the dogs eat the crumbs that fall from their masters' table." Then Jesus answered her, "O woman, great is your faith! Be it done for you as you desire." And her daughter was healed instantly.

(Matthew 15:21–28)

MANY PEOPLE CAN'T FIGURE THIS PASSAGE OUT. WHY IS JESUS, who preaches love, so insulting to this woman? Many sermons will gloss over Jesus' apparent harshness. The passage troubles us, and we would like to avoid it. What *is* going on here?

It is important to note the setting. Jesus has taken his disciples to these pagan cities (in present-day Lebanon) outside of Herod's jurisdiction. Perhaps he wants to avoid attention and persecution, to have time and quiet to teach his disciples.

And what happens? A pagan woman cries out to him when she recognizes him; she needs help for her daughter. Note a very interesting fact: The woman calls Jesus the Son of David. A pagan is acknowledging what some of Jesus' own people refuse to accept—that he is the Messiah.

Yet Jesus is silent. The disciples seem to intercede for the woman, but it is evident that their only motive is to get rid of her. Jesus finally says, "I came only for the people of Israel."

I often think of this woman, desperate for her child's deliverance and surrounded by a hostile group. Perhaps she is brave enough to take the negative reactions of those around her because she has some faith: She knows that if anyone can heal her daughter, it would be this Jew!

If I were that woman, I might turn away in anger and despair. But when a mother is desperate, nothing will stop her. She further humbles herself by kneeling down in the dirt and pleading for Jesus' help. He looks at her and says, "It is not fair to take the food for the Jews and give it to the dogs [you pagans]." It is an appalling insult. But look at her humble response (anything for her child): "But, sir, even the dogs eat the crumbs that fall from their masters' table."

Now, Jesus must be looking at the woman with great love. He has severely tested her to see if her faith is real, and she has passed with flying colors. How great in turn is her joy at seeing her daughter delivered from the evil that has plagued her.

Down through the ages this woman is known to the people of God as a woman of great faith. When I go to live in the house of the Father, I want to spend time with her, for she inspires me.

Do you persevere in prayer? Do you know who Jesus is? If he seems silent, do you ask him again and again for what you need? Do you humble yourself and continue to cry out for mercy for yourself and those you love?

Saint Josemaría Escrivá, in his little book *The Way*, wrote: "Persevere in prayer. *Persevere, even when your efforts seem sterile.* Prayer is *always* fruitful."[1]

21

. . .

DECLARING JESUS

Now when Jesus came into the district of Caesarea Philippi, he asked his disciples, "Who do men say that the Son of man is?" And they said, "Some say John the Baptist, others say Elijah, and others Jeremiah or one of the prophets." He said to them, "But who do you say that I am?" Simon Peter replied, "You are the Christ, the Son of the living God." And Jesus answered him, "Blessed are you, Simon Bar-Jona! For flesh and blood has not revealed this to you, but my Father who is in heaven. And I tell you, you are Peter, and on this rock I will build my Church, and the gates of Hades shall not prevail against it. I will give you the keys of the kingdom of heaven, and whatever you bind on earth shall be bound in heaven, and whatever you loose on earth shall be loosed in heaven." Then he strictly charged the disciples to tell no one that he was the Christ.

(Matthew 16:13–20)

JESUS LED HIS DISCIPLES CAREFULLY THROUGH A PROCESS THAT each of us must follow. First he, in essence, asked them, "What are others saying about me? Who do they think I am?" In a sense that was an easy question to answer; they only had to report what they had heard. They knew that many people thought he was very good, even one of the greatest prophets come back to Earth. Jesus listened to all this, and in the listening he probably received a sense of the level of personal faith of each of those in front of him. I wonder if he was priming the pump for the one crucial question.

Then Jesus asked that question: Who do *you* say that I am? Perhaps some of his disciples looked down at their feet or off into the distance. Perhaps they were not yet ready to declare themselves. But Peter was ready to acknowledge Jesus for who he was: "You are the Christ, the son of the living God!"

And where are you? Have you clearly declared what you believe about God, about the Father, about your Savior and Lord, about the Holy Spirit? Have you declared it to God and to yourself?

Years ago I was at a youth conference at Franciscan University in Steubenville, Ohio. At the Saturday evening session of the weekend conference, the speaker concluded his talk by asking the young people, "Have you ever made a personal declaration of faith in Christ publicly? Have you openly declared your allegiance to him?"

There were a couple thousand young people under a tent on a hillside, and still you could hear a pin drop. It seemed that collectively all the young and the adults present were holding their breath.

The speaker continued, "I want to give you an opportunity tonight to declare your personal commitment to Jesus Christ."

No one spoke; no one moved. The silence continued for five minutes.

I thought, OK, that's enough. It's a good idea, but these people are clearly not ready for this public statement of their faith. Let's move on.

Five more minutes went by. Most of the adults were restless. Still the speaker waited, and I am sure he was praying. At about the eleven-minute mark (by my watch), a young man stood up and said, "Jesus Christ is my Lord and Savior."

Again it was quiet, and then a second young man shouted out, "Jesus Christ is the Son of God and my Savior!" Then a young woman, then an adult. It went on and on until every single person there, as far as I could see, had made a public commitment of his or her faith. Never have I witnessed such a life-changing moment for so many.

Today we need courageous youth and adults to declare their faith openly. It took courage for Peter to do it that day in Caesarea Philippi; it takes courage for each of us to stand before our peers—in schools, in parish meetings, in township and county political meetings—and declare whose disciples we are, as we face very challenging social and political issues as well as religious ones.

Those young people at Franciscan University were in an ideal situation to declare their commitment to Christ simply and straightforwardly out loud. Yet surely we, too, can do so, if only in the privacy of our own homes. Declare out loud your allegiance to Christ. That declaration of the truth, even when "only" the kingdom of heaven can hear, will strengthen you. It will open you to grace and power, clear out fuzzy thinking and wash you clean from fear and confusion.

Then ask God, how do I declare my faith in you in such and such a situation? Rely on his Spirit.

Finally, ask Saint Peter's intercession, that you may have courage to speak as he did: "You are the Christ, the Son of the living God." Then hear God say to you: "Blessed are you, (insert your name), for flesh and blood has not revealed this to you, but my Father who is in heaven." Take your place in the ranks of those who declare their faith and do not turn back (see Hebrews 10:39).

22

Take the Cross

From that time Jesus began to show his disciples that he must go to Jerusalem and suffer many things from the elders and chief priests and scribes, and be killed, and on the third day be raised. And Peter took him and began to rebuke him, saying, "God forbid, Lord! This shall never happen to you." But he turned and said to Peter, "Get behind me, Satan! You are a hindrance to me; for you are not on the side of God, but of men."

Then Jesus told his disciples, "If any man would come after me, let him deny himself and take up his cross and follow me. For whoever would save his life will lose it, and whoever loses his life for my sake will find it. For what will it profit a man, if he gains the whole world and forfeits his life? Or what shall a man give in return for his life? For the Son of man is to come with his angels in the glory of his Father, and then he will repay every man for what he has done."

(Matthew 16:21–27)

JESUS HAS JUST SPOKEN POWERFULLY TO PETER, ENTRUSTING TO him the pastoral care of God's people. He blesses him, telling him that his declaration of Jesus' divinity has been given him by the Father. "Flesh and blood has not revealed this to you" (Matthew 16:17). Pretty heady stuff! You can imagine, can't you, the thoughts and feelings that must rush upon Peter. Jesus chose *me*?

And yet, right then, Jesus chooses to tell the disciples that he is about to suffer and die. Peter can't take that in. What is Jesus saying? This is the Messiah; he is going to save his people. The years of suffering and slavery and turmoil are over. That he would suffer and die seems impossible. This doesn't fit Peter's frame of reference—nor that of the other disciples, for that matter. So Peter corrects Jesus, telling him not to talk like that.

Jesus shatters Peter's way of thinking. "Get behind me, Satan." In other words, "Peter, stop tempting me." Peter is not thinking from God's perspective but from man's. Peter has to take on the mind of Christ. He needs deeper conversion.

And so it is for us. We have to take on God's way of thinking—God's priorities, God's agenda—through his Word and the teaching of the Church. We have to make our own the paradoxes of the gospel. To do that we have to die to our own way of thinking, just as Peter did.

Let's consider the Lord's words in reference to the world's priorities, which so often influence our agenda.

• *Deny yourself!* This does not, first of all, refer to giving up candy or coffee or whatever happens to be your favorite indulgence. To deny self is to give up whatever in you is selfish, self-centered, self-concerned. Take a long hard look at how you value life, people, possessions, power, titles. What is most important to you? Could you give that up so that Christ could reign more in your life?

• *Take up your cross!* What is the cross for you at this time in your life? Is it in the area of relationships or health or money?

Is it dreams that haven't materialized? the death of a loved one? Loneliness? Is it an area of sin or addiction? What are you carrying right now that weighs you down?

So often we rebel against our crosses. I am not talking about the legitimate pursuit of whatever will help to alleviate our suffering. What I am talking about is anger, bitterness and hopelessness in the face of suffering. The Christian walk has no place for these.

Jesus is telling you to take up your cross, and he will give you the grace to carry it, if you ask. Don't try to get rid of the cross or hide it. Don't get angry about it or give in to hopelessness. Pick up your cross, embrace it and follow Jesus. He tells us that his yoke is easy, and his burden is light (see Matthew 11:28).

• *Follow me.* When we follow Jesus with our crosses, he helps us carry them. We are not alone. The cross you carry may be the means by which you find a close relationship with the Lord. And the joy that comes from that relationship, no one will take from you.

To pursue peace and happiness according to the world's standards, at any price, is to follow the road to perdition. Only taking up your cross and following Jesus will bring true peace and happiness. It is the paradox of the Good News: Die in order to live; light will come out of darkness; sadness will turn to joy.

Don't let the world sell you a false bill of goods. Peter had to change his way of thinking. So do we!

23

. . .

WORK IT OUT

"If your brother sins against you, go and tell him his fault, between you and him alone. If he listens to you, you have gained your brother. But if he does not listen, take one or two others along with you, that every word may be confirmed by the evidence of two or three witnesses. If he refuses to listen to them, tell it to the Church; and if he refuses to listen even to the Church, let him be to you as a Gentile and a tax collector. Truly, I say to you, whatever you bind on earth shall be bound in heaven, and whatever you loose on earth shall be loosed in heaven. Again I say to you, if two of you agree on earth about anything they ask, it will be done for them by my Father in heaven. For where two or three are gathered in my name, there am I in the midst of them."

(Matthew 18:15–20)

BEFORE YOU READ THIS MEDITATION, REFER TO THE COMMENtary on Matthew 5:17–37 (chapter six in this book). That passage teaches that if you have sinned against your brother, *you* should *go to him.* The initiative is yours.

Now look at the passage above. It clearly says that if someone hurts you, *you* are to go and seek to rectify the situation. Whether you have offended another or been offended, the initiative is yours!

Can you imagine what life would be like if we all heeded this direction? So often when someone has offended us, we figure that the initiative to straighten it out should be theirs. But that is not what Scripture counsels. Our minds need conversion!

You see, Jesus so values our relationships that he wants all parties to make haste to heal them when difficulties occur. He wants our relationships to be signs of love and unity, signs of God's presence. We should meet "on the way."

One time when I realized that I needed to apologize to someone for something I had said. I tried repeatedly to call that person, but her line seemed to be perpetually busy. When I finally reached her, she seemed startled to hear my voice. Apparently she had been trying to call me at the same times I was trying to reach her!

Already some heat had gone from the offense, because it was obvious that we both valued the other and wanted to resolve the issue. Before we talked about the details, I said simply, "Will you forgive me?" And she responded, "Yes, of course, I forgive you." Simple, straightforward, direct. Then we talked about what to do or not do in the future to safeguard our relationship.

Some challenging relationships will not be resolved as quickly as the one I described. (My example sounds like a textbook example, but I assure you that it happened that way.) However, if you follow the principles outlined here, you will be following God's Word, which will bring blessing in itself and will at least help move things in the right direction.

If those steps don't resolve things, then in the spirit of the teaching, see if you can agree on one person to meet with both of you, to listen to the disagreement and to aid you in bringing resolution and peace. If it is a serious moral matter, take it to a pastor on whom you can both agree, if possible.

A word about forgiveness: To forgive means (1) that you will work toward letting go of all resentment, (2) that you will not speak against that person to anyone other than the person helping you reconcile and (3) that you will pray sincerely for God's blessings upon the other.

You may still have to deal with emotional squalls in your heart. Don't speak or act out of them. Acknowledge them, and give them to *God* for healing. Let the truth, not your feelings, govern your relationships! God wants your emotional life to serve you and your relationships, not damage or destroy them.

Reconciliation takes grace and humility, time, effort, wisdom and prayer. If you sincerely ask God for help in this area, he will give it to you. If you follow God's way, you will not be disappointed.

One last warning: Don't gossip. Sometimes when we're hurt we want people to sympathize with us, but their interpretations or advice can add fuel to the fire, primarily because they have only heard our side of the story.

A woman came to Saint John Vianney and confessed the gossip in which she had participated. For her penance he told her to take a feather pillow and tear it open, dumping the feathers out of her upstairs window. She did this and then reported back to her confessor.

"Now," Saint John said, "go and pick up all the feathers."

"Why, that's impossible," she retorted. "The wind has scattered them far and wide."

And so it is with gossip. The rumors, half-truths and personal opinions we utter are scattered in the wind, and we can never repair all the damage.

For further reading on the topic of reconciliation, I suggest the Letter of James and my pamphlet *Why Forgive?*[1]

24

Forgive From the Heart

Then Peter came up and said to him, "Lord, how often shall my brother sin against me, and I forgive him? As many as seven times?" Jesus said to him, "I do not say to you seven times, but seventy times seven.

"Therefore the kingdom of heaven may be compared to a king who wished to settle accounts with his servants. When he began the reckoning, one was brought to him who owed him ten thousand talents; and as he could not pay, his lord ordered him to be sold, with his wife and children and all that he had, and payment to be made. So the servant fell on his knees, imploring him, 'Lord, have patience with me, and I will pay you everything.' And out of pity for him the lord of that servant released him and forgave him the debt. But that same servant, as he went out, came upon one of his fellow servants who owed him a hundred denarii; and seizing him by the throat he said, 'Pay what you owe.' So his fellow servant fell down and besought him, 'Have patience with me, and I will pay you.' He refused and went and put him in prison till he should pay the debt. When his fellow servants saw what had taken place, they were greatly distressed, and they went and reported to their lord all that had taken place. Then his lord summoned him and said to him, 'You wicked servant! I forgave you all that debt because you pleaded with me; and should not you have had mercy on your fellow servant, as I had mercy on you?' And in anger his lord delivered him to the jailers, till he should pay all his debt. So also my heavenly Father will do to every one of you, if you do not forgive your brother from your heart."

(Matthew 18:21–35)

THE KING FORGIVES HIS SERVANT AN ENORMOUS DEBT. THEN that same servant is asked to forgive a much smaller amount owed him. Now the shoe is on the other foot, and look at his attitude!

It is easy for us to say, "What an unjust servant!" But look at him again. Can you see yourself in that servant?

Look for a moment at what God has forgiven you. Think of the countless times you have experienced the forgiveness of God in confession. And God not only forgives but forgets! "I am He who blots out your transgressions for my own sake, and I will not remember your sins" (Isaiah 43:25). "I have swept away your transgressions like a cloud, and your sins like mist; return to me, for I have redeemed you" (Isaiah 44:22).

Jesus paid the ultimate price to free us from the eternal punishment our sins deserve. And on top of that, he continues to forgive our everyday transgressions. As long as we sincerely repent, he wipes our sins away!

But Jesus also tells us, "Love one another as I have loved you" (John 15:12). Part of that love is a willingness to forgive others who commit sins against us—not only once but again and again. Do we?

Someone once said, "God is a fool; his love is foolish!" The idea is that we take advantage of God, lightly receiving his forgiveness with no intention of changing our ways and no resolution to forgive as we have been forgiven. Still God is willing to be thought of as foolish in the hope that the light will finally dawn on us, that we will realize that his love is worth any change we may have to go through.

So if you want to learn to forgive others, start by receiving the mercy God has toward you. Cherish God's lavish gift of forgiveness by sincerely changing your ways. As you experience and grow in gratitude for God's forgiveness, you will be more merciful toward others.

Many of you are in a position of authority over others—perhaps as a parent, employer or superior—and on occasion you need to responsibly ask for and expect change from a subordinate. Be sure that your forgiveness for each particular wrongdoing comes from your heart. Don't catalogue every offense the person has committed in the past. Genuinely forgive, do not harbor resentment. Pray for the person, that he or she may have strength to change. Discipline your mind to focus on the person's good qualities. God never commands anything without giving us all the grace we need. We just have to decide to obey him.

Forgiving from the heart costs a lot. But God will never be outdone in generosity!

Is God Fair?

"For the kingdom of heaven is like a householder who went out early in the morning to hire laborers for his vineyard. After agreeing with the laborers for a denarius a day, he sent them into his vineyard. And going out about the third hour he saw others standing idle in the market place; and to them he said, 'You go into the vineyard too, and whatever is right I will give you.' So they went. Going out again about the sixth hour and the ninth hour, he did the same. And about the eleventh hour he went out and found others standing; and he said to them, 'Why do you stand here idle all day?' They said to him, 'Because no one has hired us.' He said to them, 'You go into the vineyard too.' And when evening came, the owner of the vineyard said to his steward, 'Call the laborers and pay them their wages, beginning with the last, up to the first.' And when those hired about the eleventh hour came, each of them received a denarius. Now when the first came, they thought they would receive more; but each of them also received a denarius. And on receiving it they grumbled at the householder, saying, 'These last worked only one hour, and you have made them equal to us who have borne the burden of the day and the scorching heat.' But he replied to one of them, 'Friend, I am doing you no wrong; did you not agree with me for a denarius? Take what belongs to you, and go; I choose to give to this last as I give to you.

Am I not allowed to do what I choose with what belongs to me? Or do you begrudge my generosity?' So the last will be first, and the first last."

(Matthew 20:1–16)

ONE OF THE MOST IMPORTANT ISSUES IN PERSONAL DEVELOPment is how we deal with envy and jealousy. This area of sin damages our souls and plagues our society—big time!

This householder was just: He gave his workers what he promised. All would have been well, but later in the day the generous householder hired others for the same wage he was giving those who worked all day. Perhaps he saw their need: You work, you eat; you don't work, you don't eat. The householder was just with the first laborers and generous and compassionate with those who came later.

When we were children, we often complained when someone received more than we did. We were too young to see the bigger picture, to understand why parents and teachers acted as they did. We often said, "Unfair, unfair." Sometimes we retain that narrow mentality as adults. We feel that justice and compassion can't work together—but they can!

Think of the times when your sins deserved great punishment and you were given another chance. Think, on the other hand, of the times when you experienced God's correction. If you are a mature person, you said, "Well, I deserved that. Better not do that again." We learn from both mercy and justice, and as we mature we become grateful for both. God *is* justice, and God *is* mercy.

In this parable the Lord is teaching us a lesson about envy. Give it up! Repent! You are not the judge! You don't see the whole picture. You have no inside track into how God is dealing with another person. Maybe that person needs mercy more than correction.

The only soul we even have a chance of knowing is our own. So let us put aside any envy and jealousy. Let us ask God for the grace to rejoice with others in their good fortune. And let us pray that we may see God's plan in the circumstances of our own lives. We know that our heavenly Father will grant us exactly what will bring us into union with him.

Ask yourself: How do I handle it when others are praised, receive honor or are compensated in some way for outstanding work? Do I rejoice with them? Do I thank God for that person's blessing?

Envy and jealousy bind and embitter. If you find yourself going down that road, decide to turn around right away. Look to God; recount all the ways he cares for you. Choose to focus on those blessings. When you do, envy and jealousy will shrivel, because there is nothing to feed them.

26

A REAL YES

"What do you think? A man had two sons; and he went to the first and said, 'Son, go and work in the vineyard today.' And he answered, 'I will not'; but afterward he repented and went. And he went to the second and said the same; and he answered, 'I go, sir,' but did not go. Which of the two did the will of his father?" They said, "The first." Jesus said to them, "Truly, I say to you, the tax collectors and the harlots go into the kingdom of God before you. For John came to you in the way of righteousness, and you did not believe him, but the tax collectors and the harlots believed him; and even when you saw it, you did not afterward repent and believe him."

(Matthew 21:28–32)

WHEN I WAS TEACHING HIGH SCHOOL A NUMBER OF YEARS AGO, I was given the task of creating a curriculum for freshman boys and girls who were barely making it academically. In the same year I was given the task of creating an English curriculum for students who were succeeding off the charts academically.

The poorer students would say no to almost anything I suggested. They had failed a lot; why be exposed to more humiliation? Every once in a while a student would come back to me and say, "I'll try, if you'll show me." Again and again I marveled at the *nos* that became *yeses* and the *yeses* that became victories.

The gifted students, on the other hand, would immediately say yes to what I asked, eager for the challenge. But often they would get too busy, too interested in something of their own choosing, to benefit from what I recommended. Some did this enough that I began to expect their initial *yeses* to be in effect *nos* somewhere down the line. After a year of this, I found that I trusted the *yes* of the poorer student more than that of the gifted one.

Now, parables as well as my homespun example here are drawn with big strokes. They don't take into account all the *nos* and *yeses* of both groups. But the experience did stay with me, and it made me make of 2 Corinthians 1:18–20 a kind of motto for myself, especially verses 19–20: "Jesus Christ…was not Yes and No; but in him it is always Yes. For all the promises of God find their Yes in him."

I want to be like Jesus, with a *yes* to the Father's will, always depending on the grace of his Spirit to maintain that *yes* through thick and thin. And I know that even if my *yes* begins with a *no*, God will, in his mercy, reward my *yes* when eventually I yield to him. God always looks at the heart and rewards the struggle, no matter how many attempts it takes to embrace his way.

Back in that high school classroom, I had one hurting young man pull a switchblade from his pocket and open it as I leaned over his desk to correct his paper. Our eyes met, and I saw the pain, the disillusionment, the fear of humiliation. Picking up the knife to the shouts of the other boys, I asked him to teach me how to use it. He was so startled that he actually began doing that.

As the other boys laughed (the girls were silent), I leaned down and whispered to him, "Never will I embarrass you by correcting your paper publicly." He nodded, finished instructing me on the use of the knife and then put it away.

In the following days what had been his *no* up to that point became a resounding *yes*. He had received mercy when he could have been severely punished. God is like that with us. He will wait with patience and love until our no becomes a *yes!*

27

CRUCIAL QUESTIONS

"Hear another parable. There was a householder who planted a vineyard, and set a hedge around it, and dug a wine press in it, and built a tower, and leased it to tenants, and went into another country. When the season of fruit drew near, he sent his servants to the tenants, to get his fruit; and the tenants took his servants and beat one, killed another, and stoned another. Again he sent other servants, more than the first; and they did the same to them. Afterward he sent his son to them, saying, 'They will respect my son.' But when the tenants saw the son, they said to themselves, 'This is the heir; come, let us kill him and have his inheritance.' And they took him and cast him out of the vineyard, and killed him. When therefore the owner of the vineyard comes, what will he do to those tenants?" They said to him, "He will put those wretches to a miserable death, and let out the vineyard to other tenants who will give him the fruits in their seasons."

Jesus said to them, "Have you never read in the Scriptures:

'The very stone which the builders rejected
has become the cornerstone;
this was the Lord's doing,
and it is marvelous in our eyes'?

Therefore I tell you, the kingdom of God will be taken away from you and given to a nation producing the fruits of it."

(Matthew 21:33–43)

THERE ARE MANY, MANY LESSONS TO BE DRAWN FROM THIS parable. It is apparent that Jesus knows that some of the Jews, especially those in authority, are troubled by him, wanting to do away with him. At the same time the leaders realize that he is very popular, and they don't want to hurt him in a way that will turn the crowds against them. What to do?

Jesus knows their thoughts. Through the parable he tells them that God made the Jews his chosen people, providing for them in every way. But they strayed from him, disobeying his commands. So he sent his prophets to warn them and bring them back to himself, and they rejected those prophets. Finally, Jesus tells them, he sent his own Son (Jesus has not so clearly declared himself yet for who he is). Him they also will kill.

Jesus looks at this crowd and asks, "What would you do?" The crowd fails to understand that he is speaking about them, and so they glibly say, "Oh, the owner should come, kill them for their betrayal and give the vineyard to others who will care for it according to the owner's wishes."

Jesus must have looked at the crowd with great sorrow for their tremendous blindness. He says, "Yes, God will take this kingdom from you and give it to those who have put their faith in me."

Sometimes people interpret this passage narrowly, stating that the Jews would no longer be the chosen people because they failed to recognize the Messiah. The Christians, they say, are now the chosen people. I don't think so! Jesus came and suffered and died for all. All those who put their faith in him, of whatever tribe or tongue or people or nation, have the opportunity to receive him and inherit the kingdom. And all those who do not have faith, who reject his Word, will not receive the kingdom.

So once again the question is before us: Do you believe that Jesus Christ is the Son of God, sent by the Father, who lived on this earth, suffered and died for us that we might have eternal life? Is your life in accord with your beliefs? If not, why not? What are you doing about it? Your eternal destiny depends on your answers and your decisions.

28

Come to the Feast!

And again Jesus spoke to them in parables, saying, "The king-dom of heaven may be compared to a king who gave a mar-riage feast for his son, and sent his servants to call those who were invited to the marriage feast; but they would not come. Again he sent other servants, saying, 'Tell those who are invited, Behold, I have made ready my dinner, my oxen and my fat calves are killed, and everything is ready; come to the marriage feast.' But they made light of it and went off, one to his farm, another to his business, while the rest seized his ser-vants, treated them shamefully, and killed them. The king was angry, and he sent his troops and destroyed those murderers and burned their city. Then he said to his servants, 'The wed-ding is ready, but those invited were not worthy. Go there-fore to the streets, and invite to the marriage feast as many as you find.' And those servants went out into the streets and gathered all whom they found, both bad and good; so the wedding hall was filled with guests.

"But when the king came in to look at the guests, he saw there a man who had no wedding garment; and he said to him, 'Friend, how did you get in here without a wedding garment?' And he was speechless. Then the king said to the attendants, 'Bind him hand and foot, and cast him into the outer darkness, where there will be weeping and gnashing of teeth.' For many are called, but few are chosen."

(Matthew 22:1–14)

THERE ARE A NUMBER OF NATIONS IN THE WORLD THAT HAVE very strict codes of hospitality that cannot be violated without repercussions. (The United States would do well to raise its standards, for in many areas we have lost even a modicum of politeness. But that is material for another occasion!) Jesus' audience understood and abided by similarly strict standards of hospitality. They would have been astounded—even enraged—at the shameful and dramatic break of the code of hospitality in this story. The flimsy excuses offered for refusing the king's invitations would be a great insult to the king and to his son. Killing the bearers of the invitations would be outrageous.

Because of their pride, Jesus' audience could not see that he was describing them! The Father sent the Son, but the Son's invitation to the kingdom would be refused, scorned, mocked and ridiculed. People had other things to do; they couldn't be bothered listening to Jesus. Many who did listen did it only to find fault.

In the parable the king decides to send his remaining servants out into the highways and byways to bring in any who will come. We are among these. Do we take the invitation seriously? Do we see its importance and put everything else in second place to the worship of God and obedience to his call? How carefully do we listen to the Lord's invitations as he guides us through life?

And do we have on our wedding garment, which is the grace of baptism? Is it beautiful or soiled?

I find myself reflecting on what happened to a friend many years ago. He was married with several children, successful in business and solid in his Christian faith. One morning he was on his way to work, with coffee in hand, listening to the local radio station, when a tractor trailer going the other way went out of control. The truck crashed through the median and instantly killed my friend.

That friend was doing ordinary things on an ordinary day, and a split second later he was standing before God rendering an account for his life. Are you ready to enter the marriage feast? If God calls you to him today, will you be ready?

29

. . .

GIVE TO GOD

Then the Pharisees went and took counsel how to entangle him in his talk. And they sent their disciples to him, along with the Herodians, saying, "Teacher, we know that you are true, and teach the way of God truthfully, and care for no man; for you do not regard the position of men. Tell us, then, what you think. Is it lawful to pay taxes to Caesar, or not?" But Jesus, aware of their malice, said, "Why put me to the test, you hypocrites? Show me the money for the tax." And they brought him a coin. And Jesus said to them, "Whose likeness and inscription is this?" They said, "Caesar's." Then he said to them, "Render therefore to Caesar the things that are Caesar's, and to God the things that are God's." When they heard it, they marveled; and they left him and went away.

(Matthew 22:15–22)

A LITTLE KNOWLEDGE OF THE HISTORY OF JESUS' TIME WILL enrich our understanding of this passage.

Among the various parties of the Jews were those who believed that if you paid the required taxes to their enemy, then you were recognizing Rome as a legitimate authority. Some paid taxes, and some would not. Others, whom you might call fundamentalists, not only refused to pay the tax but considered armed rebellion the course to take. The Pharisees chose to pay the tax for the sake of maintaining a semblance of peace, but they believed that when the Messiah came, he would free them from their oppressors and the humiliating taxes.

So the Pharisees pose the question: If Jesus refuses to pay the tax, can they get rid of him by handing him over to the Romans? On the other hand, they wonder whether Jesus is the Messiah. Perhaps his answer will give them a hint.

Jesus dumbfounds his inquirers. He gives the criteria for the separation of church and state. On the coin is the image of Caesar, whom the Romans worship as god. Down through the centuries there have been many dictators who have sought or demanded their subjects' worship, effectively eliminating God from the picture. Daniel was cast into the lions' den for worshiping God instead of King Darius (see Daniel 6:10–28). Many of the early Christians died for their refusal to worship a civil ruler. And there are countries today where Christians are persecuted for their faith.

You and I are made in the image and likeness of God. It is he whom we worship. We bear his image, not that of an emperor or a king. We are to respect and follow the rightful orders of our duly elected officials and pray for them, but our whole heart, soul, mind and strength are given us that we may worship *God,* not man.

Give to Caesar what is Caesar's, and to God what is God's. Take a look at your own life. Are you following God's direction?

Take a look at the world we live in. Do our elected officials use this measuring rod? Do you seek to elect those who do? Only then can there be true peace in our civil society and in our hearts.

30

THE TWO GREAT COMMANDMENTS

But when the Pharisees heard that he had silenced the Sadducees, they came together. And one of them, a lawyer, asked him a question, to test him. "Teacher, which is the great commandment in the law?" And he said to him, "You shall love the Lord your God with all your heart, and with all your soul, and with all your mind. This is the great and first commandment. And a second is like it, You shall love your neighbor as yourself. On these two commandments depend all the law and the prophets."

(Matthew 22:34–40)

THE JEWISH LEADERS CONTINUE THEIR ATTEMPTS TO DISCREDIT Jesus. There were at least 613 precepts of the Jewish law, all of which had to be kept rigorously. So when the Pharisees ask Jesus which is the greatest, they are testing him. How can he choose one?

Once again it is helpful to look at the preceding verses. Jesus and the Sadducees have been dealing with questions of marriage. Who will your spouse be in the life to come if you have been married more than once (see Matthew 22:23–33)?

Many of Jesus' questioners are not really interested in sorting out such issues. They are trying to trip Jesus up, so they can fault him for being in violation of the Law. Jesus puts aside all their arguments and squabbles and goes to the heart of the matter. He tells the Sadducees the truth about the resurrection. And with the Pharisees he ignores the accumulation of minutiae that encrust the Jewish Law and goes straight to the heart of the Law: love!

Today Jesus does the same with us. Before we deal with issues like the Latin liturgy, marriage annulments, stem-cell research and abortion—all important issues—Jesus asks us, *do you love me, and do you love one another?*

To answer those questions, first ponder another question: Do you know how much God loves you? Only if you do can you return the love he deserves.

Look at the love God has for you. In John 17 Jesus prays that his followers "may know that you have...loved them even as you have loved me" and "that the love with which you have loved me may be in them, and I in them" (John 17:23, 26). The Father's love for the Son is the same love with which God loves us. Jesus prays that the love in him from the Father will be in us!

I don't know about you, but that boggles my mind. By my baptism I have been given a place in the midst of the love between the Father and the Son. I am drawn to be one with them in the love they share with each other. I am caught up in that union between Father and Son by the Holy Spirit.

I can choose to reject or ignore that love, but it is still there for me. Better that I enter into it by faith in God my Father and in his Son, Jesus, who gave his life for me, that I might fully share in that dynamic union between Father and Son. I don't want anything to keep me from drinking from the wells of life-giving water.

Once I have begun assimilating the truth of God's love through the grace of the Holy Spirit, I begin to change the way I love and care for others. The source of my love for others is not me but the love of God poured forth into me. As that love purifies me, I am more able to see his image and likeness in others. My likes and dislikes, personality conflicts, agreements and disagreements, take second place to the overwhelming love of God.

When we have submerged ourselves in God's love through daily prayer, the Eucharist and the sacrament of reconciliation, we can reach out even to our enemies with trust and with confidence that God will show us the way. We can address very "hot" issues in the Church and society, issues about which we may feel strongly, yet we can do it with kindness and respect and regard for the dignity of those who see matters differently.

Does all this involve death to self? Yes, it sure does. However, once we are submerged in the love of God, we are eager to see that love have its full effect in us and in others. We want him to rule and reign over us and through us!

31

SAY *AND* DO

Then said Jesus to the crowds and to his disciples, "The scribes and the Pharisees sit on Moses' seat; so practice and observe whatever they tell you, but not what they do; for they preach, but do not practice. They bind heavy burdens, hard to bear, and lay them on men's shoulders; but they themselves will not move them with their finger. They do all their deeds to be seen by men; for they make their phylacteries broad and their fringes long, and they love the place of honor at feasts and the best seats in the synagogues, and salutations in the market places, and being called rabbi by men. But you are not to be called rabbi, for you have one teacher, and you are all brethren. And call no man your father on earth, for you have one Father, who is in heaven. Neither be called masters, for you have one master, the Christ. He who is greatest among you shall be your servant; whoever exalts himself will be humbled, and whoever humbles himself will be exalted."

(Matthew 23:1–12)

THIS PASSAGE OF SCRIPTURE IS A VERY FORCEFUL AND CONVICTing message to those, first of all, who exercise religious authority. Your life must be in conformity with what you teach—that is, the Word of God! None of us, but most especially those in leadership, can teach one thing and do another. If you do, your words will ring increasingly hollow. People will sense, after hearing you a few times, that there is no conviction, no living reality behind your words. Only fire can set on fire!

"The Church does not live on herself but on the Gospel," stated Pope Benedict XVI, "and in the Gospel always and ever anew finds the directions for her journey. This is a point that every Christian must understand and apply to himself or herself: only those who first listen to the Word can become preachers of it. Indeed, they must not teach their own wisdom but the wisdom of God, which often appears to be foolishness in the eyes of the world (see 1 Corinthians 1:23)."[1]

This is true also for teachers and parents, for people who serve in parishes, for those who work in the pro-life movement and with other social concerns. Your life has to be in conformity with what you are calling others to do.

All of us are sinners. All of us will fail in the eyes of those we serve. But do we humbly admit our mistakes and get up and try again? Are we serving with the attitude of the Pharisees or in conformity with the meek and humble Christ?

Some years ago, on a very wintry Saturday morning, a friend was involved in a pro-life demonstration. People of the opposite view showed up and began taunting her and others committed to the protection of life. Soon insults and crude speech filled the air.

My friend prayed. Then she slipped out of the crowd, went to a nearby store and bought a bag of donuts and some coffee. She came back to the demonstration and distributed these to as many in the crowd as she could feed. The taunts lessened; eventually the crowd quieted and dispersed. I'm sure my friend's act of generosity led some to ponder their stance as they walked away.

Let us not fall into hypocrisy, saying one thing and doing another. Let's be true disciples of the Lord—in the Church, at demonstrations, in traffic, at the airport. Whether we lead or follow, let us be genuine disciples.

Cardinal John Newman prayed:

Shine through me,
and be so in me that every soul I come in contact with
may feel Thy presence in my soul.
Let them look up and see no longer me
but only Jesus![2]

32

Now Is the Time

"Then the kingdom of heaven shall be compared to ten maidens who took their lamps and went to meet the bridegroom. Five of them were foolish, and five were wise. For when the foolish took their lamps, they took no oil with them; but the wise took flasks of oil with their lamps. As the bridegroom was delayed, they all slumbered and slept. But at midnight there was a cry, 'Behold, the bridegroom! Come out to meet him.' Then all those maidens rose and trimmed their lamps. And the foolish said to the wise, 'Give us some of your oil, for our lamps are going out.' But the wise replied, 'Perhaps there will not be enough for us and for you; go rather to the dealers and buy for yourselves.' And while they went to buy, the bridegroom came, and those who were ready went in with him to the marriage feast; and the door was shut. Afterward the other maidens came also, saying, 'Lord, lord, open to us.' But he replied, 'Truly, I say to you, I do not know you.' Watch therefore, for you know neither the day nor the hour."

(Matthew 25:1–13)

MANY OF US ARE PRONE TO PROCRASTINATION: "TOMORROW, I will begin"; "Next week, I will finish that project"; "After the retreat, I will begin to pray daily"; "Maybe when I have finished school or this assignment, then I will take a good look at my life and make some changes."

Unfortunately, that tomorrow or that next week or next year never comes. Why? Because we don't value making those changes highly enough. The welfare of our immortal souls seems to fall in line behind the present and pressing concerns of daily life.

We need to put down the "tyranny of the urgent" by prayer and self-discipline. We need to bring our daily schedules before the Lord in prayer and ask the Holy Spirit to help us reprioritize.

Scripture tells us: "*Now* is the acceptable time; behold, now is the day of salvation" (2 Corinthians 6:2, emphasis mine). That means that there is grace to change now! God will help us if we are willing to yield to his discipline. We want our lamps full and burning brightly. Then, when God calls, we will be ready and waiting, eager for his return to claim us for all eternity.

Reflecting on September 11, 2001: Most likely, none of those in the towers, none of the passengers on the planes, none of the police and firemen who perished knew that they would be called that day to render an account before God. No one knew that the apparent normalcy of that morning would be shattered at 8:30 AM. Stories that have emerged among survivors assure us that some were ready to meet the Lord, but perhaps others were not.

We tend to think into the future. We think we will have time tomorrow. But we may not! *NOW* is the acceptable time to respond to God's grace, to put our houses in order.

My experience tells me that it is best to work on one area of change at a time. And that one area should be what the *Lord* wants me to work on. For "unless the LORD builds the house, those who build it labor in vain" (Psalm 127:1). What does the Lord want of you today?

33

. . .

Gifts Are for Giving

"For it will be as when a man going on a journey called his servants and entrusted to them his property; to one he gave five talents, to another two, to another one, to each according to his ability. Then he went away. He who had received the five talents went at once and traded with them; and he made five talents more. So also, he who had the two talents made two talents more. But he who had received the one talent went and dug in the ground and hid his master's money. Now after a long time the master of those servants came and settled accounts with them. And he who had received the five talents came forward, bringing five talents more, saying, 'Master, you delivered to me five talents; here I have made five talents more.' His master said to him, 'Well done, good and faithful servant; you have been faithful over a little, I will set you over much; enter into the joy of your master.' And he also who had the two talents came forward, saying, 'Master, you delivered to me two talents; here I have made two talents more.' His master said to him, 'Well done, good and faithful servant; you have been faithful over a little, I will set you over much; enter into the joy of your master.' He also who had received the one talent came forward, saying, 'Master, I knew you to be a hard man, reaping where you did not sow, and gathering where you did not winnow; so I was afraid, and I went and hid your talent in the ground. Here you have what is yours.' But his master answered him, 'You wicked and slothful servant! You knew that I reap where I have not sowed, and gather where I have not winnowed? Then you ought to have invested my money with the bankers, and at my coming I should have received what was my own with interest. So take the talent from him, and give it to him who has the ten talents. For to every one who has will more be given, and he will have abundance; but from him who has not, even what he has will be taken away. And cast the worthless servant into the outer darkness, where there will be weeping and gnashing of teeth.'"

(Matthew 25:14–30)

HERE AGAIN IS A PARABLE IN WHICH JESUS TEACHES US HOW WE should prepare for the life to come. Use what God has given you to serve others and advance the kingdom of God, he tells us. Otherwise we will be found wanting on the Day of Judgment.

We were created and placed on this earth not to be isolated individuals with no thought for the needs of others. Selfishness and greed, complacency and mediocrity, can destroy us unless we repent.

We speak a great deal today of God's love for us, and I certainly consider that topic to be of prime importance. Only when we begin to genuinely know how deeply—beyond our imagining—God loves us can we be generous and self-sacrificing. Only then can we truly love others. Let us allow that understanding to penetrate to the marrow of our bones. God is indeed a God of mercy and forgiveness.

But God is also a just God. We need to understand that if we misuse our talents, purposefully squandering the gifts God has given us, he will hold us accountable on the Day of Judgment. As I said in the last reflection: "Now is the acceptable time; behold, now is the day of salvation" (2 Corinthians 6:2). Take stock of your gifts and talents. God has loaned you these from his own life, from his own heart. Do you treasure them and use them for his glory?

This is no time to look at your neighbor and compare. God will not judge you on the number of gifts you have, neither on their kind. Whether they be gifts that benefit a few or gifts that serve the whole world, what matters is what you *do* with what God has given you.

I would hate to stand before God and realize that people did not hear the gospel, people died of cold or starvation, people were lost eternally, because I didn't play the part he called me to play. Sounds like a guilt trip, I know. But maybe a little guilt is good for us now and then: guilt that gets us up and moving, that spurs us to evaluate our lives and *do something.*

God has enormously blessed the United States of America. What are we as a nation and as individuals doing to render thanks for the gifts from his lavish hand? Are we hoarding our gifts—using them for our own benefit rather than for God's purposes?

Many years ago I taught a young man with many natural gifts, including an exceptional intellect. When he was a junior in high school, I began talking with him about his future. His talent needed extra guidance, because his drawback was self-centeredness. Everything in his life he related to what it would do or not do for him personally. While that can be a characteristic of young people in their early and middle teens, they ought to move out of that self-focus and on to "What good can I do with what I have been given?"

But no matter how many conversations I had with that young man over the two years I worked with him, he never seemed to see the value in changing or enlarging his focus. In my last conversation with him before he left for college, he said, "Sister, I am going to go to college, then to law school. I am going to be the best there is and make *big* money, so I can have and do whatever I want!"

That young man made it to the top of his class in law school. And he could have been the best lawyer in his field and made lots of money. Tragically, he died at thirty-five years of age, destroyed by alcoholism.

Burying or misusing our talents (wrong motivation, wrong goals) can have serious temporal and sometimes eternal consequences. What has God has given you? And more importantly, what are you doing with those gifts?

34

. . .

CALLED TO LOVE

"When the Son of man comes in his glory, and all the angels with him, then he will sit on his glorious throne. Before him will be gathered all the nations, and he will separate them one from another as a shepherd separates the sheep from the goats, and he will place the sheep at his right hand, but the goats at the left. Then the King will say to those at his right hand, 'Come, O blessed of my Father, inherit the kingdom prepared for you from the foundation of the world; for I was hungry and you gave me food, I was thirsty and you gave me drink, I was a stranger and you welcomed me, I was naked and you clothed me, I was sick and you visited me, I was in prison and you came to me.' Then the righteous will answer him, 'Lord, when did we see you hungry and feed you, or thirsty and give you drink? And when did we see you a stranger and welcome you, or naked and clothe you? And when did we see you sick or in prison and visit you?' And the King will answer them, 'Truly, I say to you, as you did it to one of the least of these my brethren, you did it to me.' Then he will say to those at his left hand, 'Depart from me, you cursed, into the eternal fire prepared for the devil and his angels; for I was hungry and you gave me no food, I was thirsty and you gave me no drink, I was a stranger and you did not welcome me, naked and you did not clothe me, sick and in prison and you did not visit me.' Then they also will answer, 'Lord, when did we see you hungry or thirsty or a stranger or naked or sick or in prison, and did not minister to you?' Then he will answer them, 'Truly, I say to you, as you did it not to one of the least of these, you did it not to me.' And they will go away into eternal punishment, but the righteous into eternal life."

(Matthew 25:31–46)

JESUS DETAILS FOR US HERE THE WAYS IN WHICH WE CAN PUT our talents to work as God has asked us to. Sometimes people think that they have to go to soup kitchens, prisons and so forth in order to answer God's call. It's excellent to volunteer in such ways, and all of us should look at our lives and make sure that we are serving as God has asked. But what about the young husband and father working sixty to seventy hours a week to support his family? What about the mother with small children to care for? What about the home-schooling parent? What about the person caring for an elderly parent or a disabled child or spouse?

If you are in one of these situations, you probably find your time consumed by the needs that are right in front of you. Fulfilling these responsibilities prayerfully, with trust in the Lord, *is* carrying out what Jesus has asked. You don't have to look any further for ministry. God's will is as close as the nose on your face.

Make sure you see your responsibilities that way. *They are not taking you away from serving God in some ministry.* This is God's will for you at this time in your life. You are doing as much to feed and clothe and comfort as someone at the soup kitchen or hospice or prison. Stay close to Christ; serve this relative as you would Christ.

Home ministry is often harder to accomplish than any outside ministry, because you can't get away from it. It's twenty-four/seven ministry! You also don't have the objectivity that serving strangers would give you. You are more vulnerable emotionally, and self-pity can arise. Ask God for grace to serve as he desires. When it is his will that you be in a situation like this, you can count on his grace. Ask him for it moment by moment.

"Lord, when my day comes to render an account for the way I served you in all those you placed in my life, I want to be able to render that account with joy. Help me to see you in those I care for. Increase my faith and my hope." God will hear that prayer and answer.

If God is not calling you to serve a relative or close friend, look around and offer to help somewhere. Reach out! You will not have to look far to find someone in less fortunate circumstances than you.

Mother Teresa's community once received a shipment of rice. Now, the sisters needed this food badly, as did those they served. But Mother Teresa immediately took a portion from the sisters' supply and brought it to a poor Muslim woman whose family lived close by. The woman thanked Mother Teresa for her gift, then quickly disappeared. Mother Teresa learned that the woman had gone to give some of *her* portion to another family that was even less fortunate.

Are we as generous and thoughtful, not only with our surplus but in our need?

Conclusion

. . .

WORDS TO LIVE BY

SOMEONE ONCE DESCRIBED THE BIBLE AS GOD'S LOVE LETTER to his people. God addresses his Word to all his people and to each one of us specifically. But we have to open that letter if we want to benefit from it—not just read it but contemplate it and treasure it as the Word of our Beloved. Father George Montague, a noted Scripture scholar, said to me, "If you want to understand God's Word, stand under it."

This bespeaks an attitude of reverence, of obedience, of submission. How do we cultivate this in our lives? How do we truly come "under" God's Word?

AN EXAMINATION

One practice that helped me in this regard was to read and pray through, over and over, all of Psalm 119—the longest psalm in Scripture. In fact, I dare you to memorize it. Let me share with you just a few of its verses:

If your law had not been my delight,
   I should have perished in my affliction.
I will never forget your precepts;
   for by them you have given me life.
I am yours, save me;
   for I have sought your precepts.
The wicked lie in wait to destroy me;
   but I consider your testimonies....

Oh, how I love your law!

　It is my meditation all the day.

Your commandment makes me wiser than my enemies,

　for it is ever with me.

I have more understanding than all my teachers,

　for your testimonies are my meditation.

I understand more than the aged,

　for I keep your precepts.

I hold back my feet from every evil way,

　in order to keep your word.

I do not turn aside from your ordinances,

　for you have taught me.

How sweet are your words to my taste,

　sweeter than honey to my mouth!

Through your precepts I get understanding;

　therefore I hate every false way.

Your word is a lamp to my feet

　and a light to my path....

Your testimonies are my heritage for ever;

　yes, they are the joy of my heart.

I incline my heart to perform your statutes

　for ever, to the end.

(Psalm 119:92–95, 97–105, 111–112)

THIS PSALM IS A MARVELOUS EXAMINATION OF CONSCIENCE. Don't stop with just these verses. Read the whole psalm, and see what God says to you!

　The more conformed we are to God's Word, the more docile we become. Our ears are unstopped, the scales fall from our eyes, and we can begin to see and hear in conformity with God's will. This gives the Holy Spirit freer reign in us. We grow in wisdom of heart as we remove ourselves from the sewage of this world and put ourselves under the fountain of living water. Believe me, the difference is as great as that analogy!

Oh, it is quite a battle! The world will entice you in every way possible, but the more you feed on God's Word, the more conformed you will be to the truth. You will understand things from God's perspective. You will begin to be genuinely holy.

Many years ago I had the privilege of spending a day with Mother Teresa. At one point I said to her, "Mother, what is it like for you when you come to this country and see all our wealth and our waste? That must be very difficult for you, who see the needs of the poor, the destitute every day."

She looked at me and said, "Yes, sometimes when I sit down at one of your banquet tables and they pass me a huge platter of meat, I think of my children scrambling for a grain of rice, a single grain that's fallen from the table." She paused, waved her hand a couple of times in front of her face and said, "But Jesus said never to judge, and so I do not judge." Her face, even in her old age, was beautiful to behold.

That is a person who is conformed to the Word of God. The potential is in each one of us, by the grace of baptism and confirmation, to be conformed to God's Word by the living power of the Holy Spirit. And then we can have intimacy with the Lord; we can know true peace.

RADIATE GOD'S GLORY!

As I bring to a close this book about the transforming effects of meditating on Scripture, let me emphasize one other major source of nourishment. That is, of course, the Eucharist. The Second Vatican Council recognized these two avenues of grace working together: "The Church has always venerated the divine Scriptures as she venerated the Body of the Lord, in so far as she never ceases, particularly in the sacred liturgy, to partake of the bread of life and to offer it to the faithful from the one table of the Word of God and the Body of Christ" (*Dei Verbum*, no. 21).[1]

Unfortunately, some people approach feeding on the Eucharist as merely a pious duty, a holy routine. To have God offer you his own Body and Blood to nourish and strengthen you, to have him literally give himself that you might enter into union with him, who loves you more than anyone ever could: what a gift! I find it mind-boggling that we could treat this gift with only passing attention or, worse, indifference.

When we allow God deeper access to our hearts, when we eat his Body and Blood with faith, we become healthier. We grow strong in wisdom and grace to fight the daily battle. We are equipped to fight the good fight and to be light in the darkness.

Don't miss the two enormous channels of God's grace and help, the Eucharist and his Word. Grab hold of God's power to change you through his Word; "ruminate" on the Word until you share God's perspective. And feed on the Eucharist, daily if possible, that you may be able to run the race of life with joy and win the crown of everlasting life.[2]

. . .

BIBLIOGRAPHY

Hahn, Scott and Curtis Mitch. *The Gospel of Matthew*. Robert J. Shea, trans. San Francisco: Ignatius, 2005.

The Navarre Bible: Saint Matthew's Gospel, 3rd ed. New York: Scepter, 2005.

Ratzinger, Joseph (Pope Benedict XVI). *Spiritual Thoughts: In the First Year of His Papacy*. Washington: United States Conference of Catholic Bishops, 2007.

Schönborn, Christoph Cardinal. *My Jesus: Encountering Christ in the Gospel*. Robert J. Shea, trans. San Francisco: Ignatius, 2005.

Shields, Ann. *Why Forgive*? Booklet available from Renewal Ministries, 230 Collingwood, Ann Arbor, MI 48103.

Van Thuan, Francis Cardinal Xavier Nguyen. *Five Loaves & Two Fish*. Boston: Pauline, 2003.

. . .

NOTES

INTRODUCTION: GOD'S HOLY WORD

1. George Neumayr, "Do Secularists Own Reason?" *The Catholic World Report,* March 2007, p. 1.

2. Pope John Paul II, Remarks at Sixth Extraordinary Consistory, May 21, 2001, no. 3, www.vatican.va.

3. Pope Benedict XVI, Angelus, November 6, 2005, www.vatican.va.

2. BEHOLD

1. Pope Benedict XVI, Address at the Close of the Papal Spiritual Exercises, March 11, 2006, www.vatican.va.

7. LESSONS IN LOVE

1. Cardinal Christoph Schönborn, *My Jesus: Encountering Christ in the Gospel,* Robert J. Shea, trans. (San Francisco: Ignatius, 2005), p. 69.

10. THE GOOD DOCTOR

1. *Divine Mercy in My Soul: The Diary of the Servant of God Sister M. Faustina Kowalska* (Stockbridge, Mass.: Marian Press, 1987), p. 37.

12. FEAR NOT!

1. Francis Xavier Nguyen Van Thuan, *Five Loaves & Two Fish* (Boston: Pauline, 2003), p. 54.

17. THE GREATEST TREASURE

1. Pope Benedict XVI, Homily at the Mass of the Imposition of the Pallium and Conferral of the Fisherman's Ring, April 24, 2005, www.vatican.va.

2. Pope John Paul II, *Novo Millennio Ineunte*, Apostolic Letter at the Close of the Great Jubilee of the Year 2000, no. 33 (Boston: Pauline, 2001), p. 45.

19. CALL ON THE SAVIOR

1. Augustine, *Exposition of the Psalms*, John Rotelle, ed., Maria Boulding, trans. (Hyde Park, N.Y.: New City, 2002), vol. 2, p. 111.

20. GREAT FAITH

1. Josemaría Escrivá, *The Way* (New Rochelle, N.Y.: Scepter, 1965), no. 101, p. 25, emphasis mine.

23. WORK IT OUT

1. Ann Shields, *Why Forgive?*, available from Renewal Ministries, 230 Collingwood, Ann Arbor, MI 48103.

31. SAY *AND* DO

1. Pope Benedict XVI, Address to the International Congress Organized to Commemorate the Fortieth Anniversary of *Dei Verbum*, September 16, 2005, www.vatican.va.

2. Cardinal John Henry Newman, excerpt from his poem "Radiating Christ," www.spirituality.org.

CONCLUSION: WORDS TO LIVE BY

1. Austin Flannery, trans. *Vatican Council II: The Conciliar and Post Conciliar Documents* (Northport, N.Y.: Costello, 1996), p. 762.

2. For further reading: Raniero Cantalamessa, *The Eucharist, Our Sanctification*, Frances Lonergan Villa, trans. (Collegeville, Minn.: Liturgical, 1993).